MW00386629

The Communication Jungle®

Understanding Yourself and Others

FULL COURT PRESS®

PORT TOBACCO, MD USA

The Communication Jungle
Understanding Yourself and Others

Full Court Press
9015 Katie Court
Port Tobacco, MD 20677
301-934-3250

Find us online at www.fullcourtpresspublishing.com.
To report errors, please send a note to: info@businesstrainingworks.com.

Full Court Press® is a division of Business Training Works, Inc. ®

© 2010 Business Training Works, Inc.

ISBN 13: 978-1-935425-09-0

ISBN 10: 1-935425-09-9

Table of Contents

INSTANTLY

Improve Your Communication Skills

> Do you wish that you could understand what makes others tick?

> Would you like to know what others might find difficult about communicating with you?

> Do you know how to position information for different kinds of audiences?

**TURN THE PAGE
TO FIND OUT**

Instrument Overview

Since 2003 *The Communication Jungle* has helped thousands of people improve their understanding of themselves and their relationships with others. It's fast, easy to use, and accurate.

"I think I am an LMNOP"

The Communication Jungle eliminates the "alphabet soup" of letter confusion people often face when using other style instruments. Instead, this profile connects symbols people are already familiar with to business communication concepts.

Benefits

- Understand behavior
- Learn how and when to adapt behavior
- Improve communication
- Promote appreciation of differences
- Enhance individual and team performance
- Reduce conflict

Available Formats

Online, the profile is available as a single self-rated instrument and as a multi-rater instrument. In plain English this means that one person can complete a self-assessment or many people can answer the questions in addition to the primary rater. The benefit of option two is having several views and opinions about how you relate to others. This is particularly useful if you are curious as to how your self-perceptions correspond to the perceptions of others.

This printed guide is primarily designed for use during facilitated training. However, it can be used as a self-study guide.

Overview of This Book

The beginning of this guide provides an overview of the four basic styles. The second segment is a paper-based assessment. The third section outlines the strengths and opportunities of the styles. Finally, the fourth portion of the guide contains a variety of tools for exploring aspects of the styles. This section is most useful for facilitated discussion.

Overview

FAST PACE

TASK FOCUSED

RELATIONSHIP FOCUSED

SLOW PACE

- There is no style that is better than another.
- Depending on the situation, you can adapt your style.
- Just because you prefer a style, does not mean that you necessarily display all attributes of that style.

Understanding Lions

At Their Best

- Direct
- Ambitious
- Accountable
- Results-oriented
- Assertive
- Decisive
- Confident
- Courageous
- Strong Leader
- Fair
- Risk-Taker
- Independent
- Efficient
- Intense
- Deliberate
- Achieving
- Strategic Thinkers

Lions often have the ability to take charge and make decisions. They focus on a goal and take risks in order to accomplish it. Lions are often in positions of authority. They work well independently.

At Their Worst

- Restless
- Pushy
- Argumentative
- Power-Thirsty
- Dictator
- Bad Listener
- Sarcastic
- Controlling
- Aggressive
- Impatient
- Self-Centered
- Egotistical
- Short-Tempered
- Rude
- Intolerant
- Intimidating
- Bossy
- Belligerent

When stressed, Lions overlook details in their quest to "get it done." They may push aside their own feelings and the feelings of others. This can cause tension with coworkers, family, and friends. Because of their competitive nature, drivers can sometimes be workaholics.

Key Observable Behaviors

- Makes direct eye contact.
- Moves quickly with purpose.
- Speaks forcefully and with a fast pace.
- Uses direct, bottom-line language.
- Is project-driven.
- Tells you what they want.
- Hates to lose.
- Somewhat demanding.
- May have trouble focusing for long periods of time.
- Works quickly.
- Works for fun.
- Hates to waste time.
- Would rather talk than listen.

Words

Big, better, direct, definite demand, demanding, decisive, now, strong, stronger, win, change, results, today, benefits.

Phrases

Lead, follow, or get out of the way. What's the bottom line? Don't beat around the bush? Here's the deal. What's the story? What needs to get done? I've decided. Let's not just stand around. Just do it. Make it happen.

Motivator

Directness and being in control

Greatest Fear

Being taken advantage of

Understanding Peacocks

At Their Best

- Enthusiastic
- Influential
- Persuasive
- Confident
- Self-Confident
- Energetic
- Visionary

- Adaptable
- Creative
- Sociable
- Gregarious
- Lively
- Humorous
- Optimistic

Peacocks are lively and full of excitement. Because of this, they are able to inspire and motivate others. They work at a rapid pace and are very good at using alliances and relationships to accomplish goals. Peacocks are often in high-profile positions that require them to make public presentations

At Their Worst

- Talks too much, wordy
- Flighty
- Irresponsible
- Late
- Frivolous
- Inaccurate
- Superficial
- Pollyanna syndrome

- Oversells himself/herself
- Inattentive to details
- Impulsive
- Manipulative
- Hyper
- Immature
- Careless
- Silly

When stressed, Peacocks may communicate their feelings with extra intensity – criticizing and acting out toward others. Peacocks can seem overwhelming to those with less assertive styles. When charged up about an idea, Peacocks often overlook details in order to "sell" their position.

Key Observable Behaviors

- Speaks quickly with lots of physical animation and voice inflection.
- Works quickly.
- High energy level and enthusiasm.
- Hates details.
- Starts lots of projects. Finishes few.
- Full of ideas.
- Adapts well to change.
- Excitement seeker.
- Uses persuasive language.
- Has a wide range of facial expressions.
- Acts enthusiastically in most situations.
- Outgoing and meets people easily.
- Noticeable highs and lows.

Words
Fun, everybody, exciting, awesome, fantastic, feel, joy, inspiring, positive, sensational, thrilling, wonderful, terrific.

Phrases
Isn't this fun. It will be fun. Everybody is going. Let's do it together. I feel your pain. It's the latest thing. You'll look great. This looks good. I'll show you. I've had enough.

Motivator
Recognition

Greatest Fear
Social rejection and looking stupid in front of others

Understanding Doves

At Their Best

- Self-Controlled
- Easygoing
- Predictable
- Patient
- Stable
- Unselfish
- Diplomatic
- Helpful

- Caring
- Nurturing
- Likeable
- Cooperative
- Relaxed
- Supportive
- Group-Oriented
- Steady

Doves are generally good listeners and people that others tend to rely on for support. They are good collaborators who do well as members in a team environment. Doves are often in positions that allow them to help other people.

At Their Worst

- Deadline Problems
- Stubborn
- Too Lenient
- Dislikes Change
- Avoids Decision-Making
- Accepts Mediocre Work
- Procrastinate
- Whiney

- Martyr
- Withdrawn
- Dependent
- Shy
- Meek
- Easily Intimidated
- Clingy
- Too Sensitive

Doves often have trouble asserting themselves and making decisions in a timely manner. Generally, they will avoid conflict with other people. Unfortunately, this means that they don't always get what they want and can harbor resentment. This can lead to stress with others.

Key Observable Behaviors

- Has pleasant facial expressions.
- Makes frequent eye contact.
- Uses controlled, non-dramatic gestures.
- Uses supportive and encouraging language.
- Avoids drawing attention to themselves.
- Sensitive to others' feelings.
- Seeks others' approval before acting.
- Dislikes friction and conflict.
- Speaks in soft tones at an even pace.
- Usually listens more than talks.
- Less likely to try new things.
- Is patient in most situations.

Words
Nice, kind, sensitive, traditional, same, teamwork, unity, stable, secure, safe, protected, usual, customary.

Phrases
I really care about you. I don't want to hurt anyone's feelings, I don't like change just for the sake of change. Let's work together. What does everyone else think? Take your time. Think about it.

Motivator
Traditional practices

Greatest Fear
Loss of stability

Understanding Turtles

At Their Best

- Conscientious
- Systematic
- Diplomatic
- Accurate
- Perfectionist
- Detail-oriented

- Logical
- Factual
- Well-organized
- Analytical

Turtles generally have a natural inclination toward fact finding and problem solving. They have the patience to examine each and every detail and to come up with logical and sound solutions. Often, those with this behavioral pattern will find themselves in positions that require a great deal of detail.

At Their Worst

- Avoids Controversy
- Picky-Picky-Picky
- Critical
- Habitual
- Nagging
- Unforgiving
- Slow
- Bogged Down In Detail

- Avoids Change
- Not People-Oriented
- Avoids Making Decisions
- Pessimistic
- Narrow-Minded
- Obsessive
- Isolating
- Humorless

Turtles often place facts and accuracy ahead of feelings and people. Others may view them as cold and emotionally distant. Under stress, they will over analyze and avoid making decisions. Some people with this pattern are uncomfortable with emotions and will avoid expressing their feelings even when it is in their best interest to do so.

Key Observable Behaviors

- Shows limited facial expression.
- Have controlled body movements and speaks in even, controlled tones.
- Use language that is precise and focuses on detail.
- Likes charts, graphs, and statistics.
- Thinks things through and considers multiple options.
- Likes privacy and working alone.

Words
Accurate, reason, think, analyze, consider, contemplate, due diligence, study, research.

Phrases
The smart thing to do is…. The right way to go about it is…. We need a "plan b." Please explain. I need time to process that information. I don't want to make a split decision. Let's weigh all of the options.

Motivator
The proper way of doing things

Greatest Fear
Criticism of his or her work

Take the Assessment

1

- Choose the area where you would like to improve communication, for example, work or home.

2

- Review the 26 groups of words presented on the following pages, and select the word from each group that is most like you and the word that is least like you.

3

- Remember that there are no right or wrong answers.

Example:

	Most	Least
Calm	(D)	d
Controlled	T	t
Daring	L	(l)
Enthusiastic	P	p

If you need the definition of a word, use the thesaurus on page 18.

MY FOCUS IS: ☒ WORK ☐ HOME

Instrument

1.		Most	Least
	Calm	D	d
	Controlled	T	(t)
	Daring	L	l
	Enthusiastic	(P)	p

2.		Most	Least
	Cautious	T	t
	Conventional	D	(d)
	Determined	(L)	l
	Life of the Party	P	p

3.		Most	Least
	Friendly	P	p
	Gentle	D	(d)
	Outspoken	L	l
	Realistic	(T)	t

4.		Most	Least
	Decisive	(L)	l
	Formal	T	t
	Soft-Spoken	D	(d)
	Talkative	P	p

5.		Most	Least
	Adventurous	L	l
	Helpful	(D)	d
	Outgoing	P	p
	Patient	T	(t)

6.		Most	Least
	Conscientious	T	t
	Direct	(L)	l
	Persuasive	P	p
	Traditional	D	(d)

7.		Most	Least
	Disciplined	T	t
	Dominant	(L)	l
	Expressive	P	p
	Lenient	D	(d)

8.		Most	Least
	Accurate	T	t
	Animated	P	(p)
	Easy-Going	D	d
	Impatient	(L)	l

9.		Most	Least
	Insistent	(L)	l
	Magnetic	P	p
	Perfectionist	T	(t)
	Tolerant	D	d

10.		Most	Least
	Brave	(L)	l
	Inspiring	P	p
	Loyal	D	d
	Structured	T	(t)

11.		Most	Least
	Cheerful	P	p
	Strong-Minded	(L)	l
	Sympathetic	D	d
	Systematic	T	(t)

12.		Most	Least
	Exacting	T	t
	Independent	(L)	l
	Joyful	P	p
	Predictable	D	(d)

13.		Most	Least
	Competitive	L	l
	Detailed	(T)	t
	Obedient	D	(d)
	Playful	P	p

14.		Most	Least
	Agreeable	D	(d)
	Precise	T	t
	Sociable	P	p
	Stubborn	(L)	l

15.

	Most	Least
Charming	P	p
Introverted	T	(t)
Obliging	D	d
Tenacious	(L)	l

16.

	Most	Least
Bold	(L)	l
Curious	T	t
High-Spirited	P	p
Modest	D	(d)

17.

	Most	Least
Amiable	D	d
Extraverted	P	p
Particular	T	(t)
Self-Starter	(L)	l

18.

	Most	Least
Careful	T	t
Confident	(P)	p
Eager	L	l
Placid	D	(d)

19.

	Most	Least
Aggressive	L	l
Optimistic	P	p
Peaceful	D	(d)
Thorough	(T)	t

20.

	Most	Least
Assertive	(L)	l
Harmonious	D	(d)
Impulsive	P	p
Tactful	T	t

21.

	Most	Least
Enchanting	P	p
Mild	D	(d)
Persistent	L	l
Private	(T)	t

22.

	Most	Least
Energetic	P	p
Forceful	(L)	l
Laid-Back	D	d
Moderate	T	(t)

23.

	Most	Least
Brisk	(L)	l
Captivating	P	p
Restrained	D	d
Satisfied	T	(t)

24.

	Most	Least
Chatty	P	p
Demanding	(L)	l
Reserved	T	(t)
Willing	D	d

25.

	Most	Least
Argumentative	L	l
Gregarious	(P)	p
Introspective	T	t
Serene	D	(d)

26.

	Most	Least
Cooperative	D	d
Egotistical	L	(l)
Influential	P	p
Logical	(T)	t

Tear or cut along the lines above and to the left to remove this portion of the book.

Then turn the page to calculate your score.

Sample Results Calculation

	Lion		Peacock		Dove		Turtle	
Extremely Strong Preference	5 or more	See Pages 29-33	10 or more	See Pages 39-43	10 or more	See Pages 49-55	(10) or more	See Pages 63-70
Strong Preference	(4) 3 2 1	See Pages 34-38	9 8 7 6 5	See Pages 44-48	9 8 7 6	See Pages 56-62	9 8 7	See Pages 71-77
Preference			4 3 2		5 4		6 5 4	
Baseline			1 0 -1		3 2 1		3 2 1	
Aversion			-2 -3 -4 -5		0 -1 (-2)		0 -1 -2	
Strong Aversion			-6 -7 -8 -9		-3 -4 -5 -6 -7		-3 -4 -5 -6	
Extremely Strong Aversion			(-10) or less		- 8 or less		-7 or less	
	Lion		Peacock		Dove		Turtle	

Find your score in each column, and circle your data point.

Next, read any of the pages referenced.

In this example the results indicate strong lion and extremely strong turtle styles.

The relevant pages are 34-38 and 63-70.

Calculate your totals for each letter and then subtract. Your capital letter total should add up to 26, and your lower case total should add up to 26.

L $\quad$ 5 $\quad$ - $\quad$ l $\quad$ 1 $\quad$ = $\quad$ 4

P $\quad$ 1 $\quad$ - $\quad$ p $\quad$ 18 $\quad$ = $\quad$ -17

D $\quad$ 1 $\quad$ - $\quad$ d $\quad$ 3 $\quad$ = $\quad$ -2

T $\quad$ 19 $\quad$ - $\quad$ t $\quad$ 4 $\quad$ = $\quad$ 15

Calculate Your Results

	Lion		Peacock		Dove		Turtle	
Extremely Strong Preference	(5 or more)	See Pages 29-33	10 or more	See Pages 39-43	10 or more	See Pages 49-55	10 or more	See Pages 63-70
Strong Preference	4 3 2 1	See Pages 34-38	9 8 7 6 5	See Pages 44-48	9 8 7 6	See Pages 56-62	9 8 7	See Pages 71-77
Preference	-1 -2 -3		4 3 (2)		5 4		6 (5) 4	
Baseline	-4 -5 -6		1 0 -1		3 2 1		3 2 1	
Aversion	-7 -8 -9		-2 -3 -4 -5		0 -1 -2		0 -1 -2	
Strong Aversion	-10 -11 -12		-6 -7 -8 -9		-3 -4 -5 -6 -7		-3 -4 -5 -6	
Extremely Strong Aversion	-13 or less		-10 or less		(-8 or less)		-7 or less	
	Lion		Peacock		Dove		Turtle	

Follow the example on the previous page to calculate your score and find the report pages related to your particular style.

If your score shows a strong or extremely strong preference for opposite styles (lion/dove or peacock/turtle) see page 78.

If you do not have an extremely strong or strong preference for at least one style, check your math. If the math is correct, see pages 79 and 80.

Calculate your totals for each letter and then subtract.

L _17_ - l _0_ = _17_

P _3_ - p _1_ = _2_

D _1_ - d _14_ = _-13_

T _5_ - t _10_ = _5_

Thesaurus

1. Accurate - authentic, careful, close, concrete, correct, defined, definite, deft, detailed, discriminating, discriminative, distinct, exact, explicit, factual, faithful, genuine, judicious, just, literal, matter-of-fact, methodical, meticulous, particular, proper, punctilious, punctual, regular, right, rigid, rigorous, scientific, scrupulous, severe, sharp, skillful, solid, specific, strict, systematic, true, unerring, unmistakable, veracious

2. Adventurous - adventuresome, audacious, bold, brave, courageous, dangerous, daredevil, enterprising, foolhardy, hazardous, headstrong, intrepid, rash, reckless, risky, temerarious, venturesome, venturous

3. Aggressive - advancing, antipathetic, assailing, attacking, barbaric, bellicose, combative, contentious, destructive, disruptive, disturbing, encroaching, hawkish, hostile, intruding, intrusive, invading, martial, offensive, pugnacious, quarrelsome, rapacious, threatening, warlike

4. Agreeable - acceptable, dandy, delicious, delightful, ducky, enjoyable, fair, far out, fine, gratifying, hunky-dory, mild, nice, peach, peachy, pleasant, pleasurable, pleasureful, ready, spiffy, swell, welcome

5. Amiable - affable, amicable, attractive, benign, breezy, buddy-buddy, charming, cheerful, clubby, complaisant, cool, copasetic, cordial, cozy, delightful, downright neighborly, easy, engaging, friendly, genial, good-humored, good-natured, gracious, home cooking, kind, kindly, lenient, lovable, mellow, mild, obliging, pleasant, pleasing, prince, pussycat, responsive, right, righteous, sociable, sweet-tempered, swell, tight, warm, warm-hearted, winning

6. Animated - activated, active, alert, animate, ardent, brisk, buoyant, dynamic, ebullient, elated, energetic, energized, enthusiastic, excited, fervent, gay, happy, passionate, peppy, quick, snappy, spirited, sprightly, vibrant, vigorous, vital, vitalized, vivacious, vivid, zealous, zestful, zingy, zippy

7. Argumentative - belligerent, combative, contentious, contrary, controversial, disputatious, factious, fire-eater, litigious, opinionated, pugnacious, quarrelsome, salty, scrappy, spiky

8. Assertive - absolute, assured, certain, confident, decided, decisive, demanding, dogmatic, domineering, emphatic, firm, forceful, forward, insistent, militant, overbearing, positive, pushy, self-assured, self-confident, strong-willed, sure

9. Bold - adventurous, assuming, audacious, aweless, bantam, courageous, daring, dauntless, enterprising, fearless, forward, gallant, heroic, intrepid, resolute, unafraid, undaunted, valiant, valorous

10. Brave - adventurous, audacious, ballsy, chin-up, chivalrous, confident, courageous, daring, dashing, dauntless, defiant, doughty, fearless, firm, foolhardy, forward, gallant, game, gritty, gutsy, hardy, heroic, hero-like, imprudent, indomitable, intrepid, lionhearted, manly, militant, nervy, plucky, reckless, resolute, skookum tumtum, spirited, spunky, stalwart, stout, strong, unabashed, unafraid, unblenching, undaunted, undismayed, unfearful, valiant, valorous, venturesome

11. Brisk - active, adroit, agile, alert, animated, bustling, busy, energetic, lively, nimble, quick, speedy, sprightly, spry, vigorous, vivacious, volant, zippy

12. Calm - aloof, amiable, amicable, civil, collected, cool-headed, detached, disinterested, dispassionate, equable, gentle, impassive, imperturbable, kind, laidback, level-headed, listless, moderate, neutral, patient, placid, pleased, poised, relaxed, restful, satisfied, sedate, self-possessed, serene, still, temperate, unconcerned, undisturbed, unemotional, unexcitable, unexcited, unflappable, unimpressed, unmoved, unruffled, untroubled

13. Captivating - alluring, appealing, attractive, bewitching, captivating, charming, compelling, delectable, delightful, enchanting, engaging, engrossing, enticing, glamorous, gripping, intriguing, irresistible, ravishing, riveting, seducing, seductive, siren, spellbinding

14. Careful - accurate, alert, apprehensive, assiduous, attentive, chary, choosy, circumspect, concerned, conscientious, conservative, cool, deliberate, discreet, exacting, fastidious, finicky, fussy, guarded, heedful, judicious, leery, meticulous, mindful, observant, particular, play safe, precise, prim, protective, provident, prudent, punctilious, regardful, religious, rigorous, scrupulous, self-disciplined, shy, sober, solicitous, thorough, thoughtful, vigilant, wary, watchful

15. Cautious - alert, all ears, cagey, calculating, chary, circumspect, considerate, discreet, forethoughtful, gingerly, guarded, heedful, judicious, leery, play safe, politic, provident, prudent, pussyfoot, safe, shrewd, tentative, think twice, vigilant, wary, watch out, watchful

16. Charming - absorbing, alluring, amiable, appealing, attractive, bewitching, charismatic, choice, cute, dainty, delectable, delicate, delightful, desirable, electrifying, elegant, enamoring, engaging, engrossing, enthralling, entrancing, eye-catching, fascinating, fetching, glamorous, graceful, infatuating, inviting, irresistible, likeable, lovable, lovely, magnetizing, nice, pleasant, pleasing, provocative, rapturous, ravishing, seducing, seductive, sweet, tantalizing, tempting, titillating, winsome

17. Chatty - communicative, conversational, familiar, friendly, gabby, garrulous, gossipy, informal, intimate, loose-lipped, loquacious, multiloquent, spontaneous, talky

18. Cheerful - airy, animated, blithe, bouncy, bright, bucked, buoyant, cheery, chipper, chirpy, contented, effervescent, enlivening, enthusiastic, gay, glad, gladsome, good-humored, good-natured, hearty, high, hilarious, hopeful, jaunty, jocund, jolly, joyful, light-hearted, lively, merry, optimistic, peppy, perky, pleasant, roseate, rosy, snappy, sparkling, sprightly, sunny, up, upbeat, vivacious, winsome, zappy, zingy, zippy

19. Competitive - aggressive, ambitious, antagonistic, at odds, competing, cutthroat, dog-eat-dog, emulous, killer, opposing, rival, streetwise, vying

20. Confident - assured, bet on, bold, brave, cocksure, convinced, courageous, dauntless, depending on, expectant, expecting, fearless, high, hopeful, intrepid, positive, presuming, presumptuous, puffed up, pushy, racked, sanguine, satisfied, secure, self-assured, self-reliant, self-sufficient, sure, trusting, unafraid, undaunted, upbeat, uppity, valiant

21. Conscientious - careful, complete, diligent, enact, exact, faithful, fastidious, fussy, heedful, meticulous, painstaking, particular, punctilious, punctual, reliable, tough

22. Controlled - assured, collected, composed, coolheaded, deliberate, detached, dispassionate, impassive, imperturbable, level-headed, nonchalant, philosophical, phlegmatic, placid, quiet, relaxed, self-controlled, self-possessed, serene, stolid, together, tranquil, unagitated, unemotional, unexcited, unflappable, unruffled

23. Conventional - accepted, accustomed, button-down, commonplace, correct, current, customary, decorous, everyday, expected, fashionable, formal, general, habitual, normal, ordinary, orthodox, plain, popular, predominant, prevailing, prevalent, proper, regular, ritual, routine, square, standard, stereotyped, straight, traditional, tralatitious, typical, usual, well-known, wonted

Thesaurus

24. Cooperative - all-around, considerate, cooperative, friendly, handy, helpful, hospitable, kind, neighborly, obliging, on deck, polite, unselfish, user-friendly

25. Curious - analytical, disquisitive, examining, impertinent, inquiring, inquisitive, inquisiturient, inspecting, interested, interfering, intrusive, investigative, meddlesome, meddling, nosy, peeping, prurient, prying, puzzled, questioning, scrutinizing, searching, snoopy, tampering

26. Daring - adventuresome, audacious, bold, brassy, brave, cheeky, cocky, courageous, crusty, fearless, fire-eater, foolhardy, forward, game, gritty, gutsy, gutty, hot shot, impudent, impulsive, intrepid, nervy, obtrusive, pizzazz, plucky, rash, reckless, salty, smart, smart-alecky, spunky, temerarious, valiant, venturesome

27. Decisive - absolute, assured, bent, certain, conclusive, crisp, critical, crucial, decided, definitive, determined, fateful, final, firm, flat out, forceful, imperative, imperious, incisive, influential, intent, litmus test, momentous, peremptory, positive, resolute, resolved, set, settled, significant, straight out, strong-minded, trenchant

28. Demanding - ambitious, backbreaker, ball-breaker, bothersome, clamorous, critical, dictatorial, difficult, exacting, exhausting, exigent, fussy, grievous, hard, imperious, importunate, insistent, nagging, onerous, oppressive, pressing, querulous, strict, stringent, taxing, tough, troublesome, trying, urgent, wearing, weighty

29. Detailed - analytic, cogent, conclusive, diagnostic, discrete, dissecting, explanatory, expository, inquiring, inquisitive, interpretive, investigative, judicious, logical, organized, penetrating, perceptive, perspicuous, precise, problem-solving, questioning, ratiocinative, rational, reasonably, scientific, searching, solid, sound, studious, subtle, systematic, testing, thorough, valid

30. Determined - bent, bent on, brick wall, buckle down, constant, decided, decisive, dogged, driven, earnest, firm, fixed, hardboiled, hell bent, intent, mean business, obstinate, on ice, pat, persevering, purposeful, resolute, resolved, serious, set, set on, settled, single-minded, solid, steadfast, strong-minded, strong-willed, stubborn, tenacious, unfaltering, unflinching, unhesitating, unwavering

31. Direct - absolute, bald, blunt, candid, categorical, downright, explicit, express, forthright, frank, man-to-man, matter-of-fact, open, outspoken, plain, plain-spoken, point-blank, sincere, straight, straightforward, talk turkey, unambiguous, unconcealed, undisguised, unequivocal, unreserved

32. Disciplined - accomplished, careful, concentrated, correct, diligent, direct, earnest, effective, enterprising, expeditious, hardworking, industrious, intent, matter-of-fact, methodical, orderly, organized, painstaking, practical, practiced, professional, purposeful, regular, routine, sedulous, serious, skillful, systematic, thorough, well-ordered, workaday

33. Dominant - ascendant, assertive, authoritative, bossy, chief, commanding, demonstrative, despotic, domineering, effective, first, foremost, governing, imperative, imperious, leading, lordly, main, master, obtaining, outweighing, overbalancing, overbearing, overweighing, paramount, powerful, predominant, preeminent, preponderant, presiding, prevailing, prevalent, principal, regnant, reigning, ruling, sovereign, superior, supreme, surpassing, transcendent

34. Eager - aggressive, agile, alert, alive, animated, assiduous, bold, brisk, bustling, busy, chipper, daring, dashing, determined, dexterous, diligent, dynamic, energetic, enlivened, enterprising, enthusiastic, eventful, fireball, forceful, forcible, fresh, frisky, hard-working, high-spirited, hyper, industrious, intense, inventive, jumping, keen, lively, nimble, perky, persevering, purposeful, pushing, quick, rapid, ready, resolute, sharp, sprightly, spry, whiz, zealous

35. Easy-Going - adjustable, all around, alterable, can do, changeable, compliant, conformable, convertible, ductile, easy-going, flexible, malleable, modelable, modifiable, plastic, pliable, pliant, putty, resilient, supple, switch hitting, tractable, variable, versatile

36. Egotistical - arrogant, big head, big-headed, bombastic, cocky, conceited, crowing, egotistic, exultant, hifalutin, hot stuff, know-it-all, loudmouth, pompous, pretentious, puffed-up, self-aggrandizing, self-applauding, smart-alecky, snooty, strutting, stuck up, swaggering, swanky, swollen-headed, vainglorious, vaunting, windbag

37. Enchanting - alluring, appealing, attractive, beguiling, bewitching, captivating, charming, delectable, endearing, enthralling, entrancing, exciting, fascinating, glamorous, intriguing, lovely, pleasant, pleasing, ravishing, seductive, siren, sirenic, winsome, witching

38. Energetic - active, aggressive, animated, breezy, brisk, demoniac, driving, dynamic, enterprising, forcible, fresh, hardy, high-powered, indefatigable, industrious, kinetic, lively, lusty, peppy, potent, powerful, red-blooded, rugged, snappy, spirited, sprightly, spry, stalwart, strenuous, strong, sturdy, tireless, tough, unflagging, untiring, vigorous, vital, vivacious, zippy

39. Enthusiastic - agog, animated, anxious, ardent, athirst, attracted, avid, bugged, buggy, concerned, crazy about, devoted, dying to, eager, earnest, ebullient, excited, exhilarated, exuberant, fanatical, fascinated, fervent, fervid, forceful, gaga, gay, gone on, gung ho, hearty, hot for, intent, keen, keyed up, lively, nuts about, nutty, obsessed, passionate, pleased, rabid, red-hot, rhapsodic, spirited, tantalized, thrilled, titillated, unqualified, vehement, vigorous, wacky, warm, wholehearted, willing, zealous

40. Exacting - burdensome, careful, critical, difficult, exigent, finicky, fussy, grievous, hard, harsh, hypercritical, imperious, nitpicking, onerous, oppressive, painstaking, particular, persnickety, picky, precise, rigid, rigorous, severe, stern, strict, stringent, taxing, tough, trying, unsparing, weighty

41. Expressive - alive, allusive, articulate, artistic, brilliant, colorful, demonstrative, dramatic, eloquent, emphatic, energetic, forcible, graphic, indicative, ingenious, lively, masterly, meaningful, mobile, moving, passionate, pathetic, pictorial, picturesque, poignant, pointed, pregnant, representative, responsive, revelatory, showy, significant, silver-tongued, spirited, stimulating, stirring, striking, strong, suggestive, sympathetic, tender, thoughtful, touching, understanding, vivid, warm

42. Extraverted - approachable, civil, communicative, cordial, easy, expansive, extrovert, friendly, genial, gregarious, informal, kind, open, sociable, sympathetic, unconstrained, unreserved, unrestrained, warm

43. Forceful - bull, cogent, commanding, compelling, constraining, convincing, dominant, dynamic, effective, electric, elemental, energetic, forcible, go-go, gutsy, manful, mighty, persuasive, pithy, potent, powerhouse, puissant, punch, punchy, steamroller, stringent, strong, take charge, take over, telling, titanic, vehement, vigorous, violent, virile, weighty

44. Formal - adulatory, affable, aristocratic, august, ceremonious, chivalrous, civil, civilized, complimentary, conventional, cultured, decorous, dignified, elegant, flattering, gallant, gracious, high-bred, imposing, lofty, lordly, obliging, polished, polite, prim, refined, stately, studied, urbane

45. Friendly - affable, affectionate, amiable, amicable, attached, attentive, auspicious, beneficial, benevolent, benign, buddy-buddy, chummy, civil, close, clubby, comradely, conciliatory, confiding, convivial, cordial, faithful, familiar, favorable, fond, fraternal, genial, good, helpful, intimate, kind, kindly, loving, loyal, neighborly, outgoing, peaceable, peaceful, propitious, receptive, sociable, solicitous, sympathetic, tender, thick, welcoming, well-disposed

46. Gentle - affable, agreeable, amiable, benign, biddable, bland, compassionate, considerate, cool, cultivated, disciplined, docile, domesticated, dove-like, easy, educated, genial, humane, kind, kindly, laid back, lenient, manageable, meek, mellow, merciful, moderate, pacific, peaceful, placid, pleasant, pleasing, pliable, quiet, soft, softhearted, sweet-tempered, sympathetic, tame, taught, temperate, tender, tractable, trained, warmhearted

47. Gregarious - affable, clubby, companionable, convivial, cordial, extroverted, fun, outgoing, sociable, social

48. Harmonious - adapted, agreeable, amicable, balanced, compatible, concordant, congenial, congruous, consonant, coordinated, cordial, correspondent, dulcet, euphonious, fraternal, harmonic, harmonizing, in accord, in chorus, in concert, in harmony, in step, in tune, like, matching, mellifluous, melodic, melodious, mix, musical, peaceful, rhythmical, silvery, similar, simpatico, sonorous, suitable, sweet-sounding, symmetrical, sympathetic, symphonic, symphonious, tuneful, unison

49. Helpful - all-around, considerate, cooperative, friendly, handy, helpful, hospitable, kind, neighborly, obliging, on deck, polite, unselfish, user-friendly

50. High-Spirited - agitated, bouncy, brash, buoyant, chipper, chirpy, effervescent, effusive, elated, excited, exhilarated, exuberant, frothy, gushing, irrepressible, vivacious, zestful, zippy

51. Impatient - abrupt, agog, antsy, anxious, appetent, ardent, athirst, avid, breathless, brusque, chafing, choleric, curt, demanding, dying to, eager, edgy, feverish, fretful, hasty, headlong, hot-tempered, impetuous, indignant, intolerant, irascible, irritable, itchy, keen, quick-tempered, restless, ripe, snappy, straining, sudden, testy, thirsty, unforbearing, unindulgent, vehement, violent

52. Impulsive - abrupt, ad lib, automatic, careless, devil-may-care, emotional, extemporaneous, flaky, hasty, headlong, impetuous, instinctive, intuitive, involuntary, mad, offhand, passionate, precipitate, quick, rash, spitball, spontaneous, sudden, swift, unconsidered, unexpected, unmeditated, unpredictable, unpremeditated, unprompted, violent, winging it

53. Independent - absolute, autarchic, autarchical, autonomous, freewheeling, individualistic, liberated, nonaligned, nonpartisan, self-contained, self-determining, self-governing, self-reliant, self-ruling, self-sufficient, self-supporting, separate, separated, sovereign, unaided, unallied, unconnected, unconstrained, uncontrolled, unregimented

54. Influential - affecting, authoritative, big gun, big wheel, controlling, dominant, effective, efficacious, famous, forcible, governing, guiding, hot dog, important, impressive, inspiring, instrumental, leading, major league, meaningful, momentous, moving, name, persuasive, potent, prominent, significant, strong, substantial, telling, touching, weighty

55. Insistent - assertive, burning, clamant, clamorous, continuous, crying, dire, dogged, emphatic, exigent, forceful, imperative, imperious, importunate, incessant, obstinate, peremptory, perseverant, persevering, persistent, pressing, reiterative, resolute, resounding, unrelenting, urgent

56. Inspiring - absorbing, affecting, captivating, charming, cheerful, cheering, clever, compelling, delightful, diverting, droll, enchanting, engaging, engrossing, enjoyable, enthralling, enticing, entrancing, exciting, fascinating, fun, funny, gas, gay, humorous, impressive, inspiring, interesting, lively, moving, piquant, pleasant, pleasurable, poignant, priceless, provocative, recreative, relaxing, restorative, riot, rousing, scream, side-splitting, stimulating, stirring, striking, thrilling, witty

57. Introspective - absorbed, analytical, attentive, brainy, calculating, cerebral, cogitative, deep, deliberative, discerning, earnest, engrossed, far-sighted, grave, intellectual, intent, keen, level-headed, logical, meditative, melancholy, museful, musing, pensive, philosophic, pondering, preoccupied, rapt, rational, reasonable, reasoning, reflecting, reflective, retrospective, ruminative, serious, sober, studious, subjective, thinking, wise, wistful

58. Introverted - afraid, apprehensive, averse, backward, bashful, cautious, chary, circumspect, conscious, coy, demure, diffident, disinclined, distrustful, fearful, hesitant, humble, indisposed, introvert, introverted, loath, loner, modest, mousy, nervous, rabbity, recessive, reluctant, reserved, reticent, retiring, self-conscious, self-effacing, shamefaced, sheepish, shrinking, skittish, suspicious, timid, unassertive, unassured, uneager, uneffusive, unresponsive, unsocial, unwilling, wallflower, wary

59. Joyful - blithesome, cheerful, cheery, delighted, doing handsprings, ecstatic, effervescent, elated, enjoyable, enraptured, expansive, festive, flipping, flying, gay, glad, gladsome, gratified, heartening, high, jocund, jolly, jovial, joyous, jubilant, lighthearted, merry, overjoyed, pleased, pleasurable, popping, rapturous, satisfied, sunny, transported, upbeat

60. Laid-Back - amenable, breezy, calm, carefree, casual, collected, complaisant, composed, devil-may-care, easy, even-tempered, flexible, hang-loose, happy-go-lucky, indolent, indulgent, informal, insouciant, lazy, lenient, liberal, low-pressure, mild, moderate, nonchalant, offhand, outgiving, patient, permissive, placid, poised, relaxed, self-possessed, serene, tolerant, tranquil, unconcerned, uncritical, undemanding, unhurried, uninhibited

61. Lenient - allowing, amiable, assuaging, assuasive, be big, benign, benignant, charitable, clement, compassionate, complaisant, compliant, condoning, easy, easy-going, emollient, excusing, favoring, forbearing, forgiving, gentle, good-natured, humoring, indulgent, kind, kindly, letting, live with, loving, merciful, mild, mollycoddling, obliging, pampering, pardoning, permitting, soft, soft shell, soft-hearted, sparing, spoiling, sympathetic, tender, tolerant, yielding

62. Life of the Party - alluring, appealing, arresting, attractive, bewitching, captivating, charismatic, charming, drawing, enchanting, entrancing, fascinating, hypnotic, inviting, irresistible, mesmerizing, pulling, seductive

63. Logical - analytic, analytical, clear, cogent, coherent, commonsensical, compelling, congruent, consequent, consistent, convincing, deducible, discerning, discriminating, extensional, fair, fly, germane, hold together, hold water, inferential, intelligent, judicious, justifiable, kosher, legit, legitimate, lucid, most likely, necessary, obvious, perceptive, perspicuous, pertinent, plausible, rational, relevant, sensible, sound, subtle, telling, valid, wash, well-organized, wise

64. Loyal - ace in, allegiant, ardent, attached, behind one, believing, come through, constant, dependable, devoted, dutiful, firm, patriotic, resolute, staunch, steadfast, steady, true, true-blue, trustworthy, trusty, unfailing, unswerving, unwavering

65. Magnetic - alluring, appealing, arresting, attractive, bewitching, captivating, charismatic, charming, drawing, enchanting, entrancing, fascinating, hypnotic, inviting, irresistible, mesmerizing, pulling, seductive

66. Mild - balmy, benign, benignant, blah, bland, breezy, calm, choice, clear, clement, cool, dainty, delicate, demulcent, easy, emollient, exquisite, faint, fine, flat, genial, ho hum, lenient, lenitive, light, lukewarm, medium, mellow, moderate, mollifying, non-irritating, nothing, nothing much, pablum, pacific, peaceful, placid, smooth, soft, soothing, sunny, temperate, tempered, tepid, untroubled, vanilla, warm, weak

67. Moderate - abstinent, balanced, bearable, calm, careful, cautious, compromising, conservative, considerate, considered, controlled, cool, deliberate, disciplined, dispassionate, equable, even, gentle, impartial, inconsiderable, inexpensive, judicious, limited, low-key, measured, middle-of-the-road, midway, mild, modest, monotonous, neutral, nonpartisan, not excessive, pacific, peaceable, pleasant, reasonable, reserved, restrained, sober, soft, steady, straight, tame, tolerable, tolerant, tranquil, untroubled

68. Modest - bashful, blushing, chaste, coy, demure, diffident, discreet, humble, lowly, meek, moderate, nice, proper, prudent, quiet, reserved, resigned, reticent, retiring, seemly, self-conscious, self-effacing, sheepish, silent, simple, temperate, timid, unassertive, unassuming, unassured, unboastful, unobtrusive, unpresuming, unpretending, unpretentious, withdrawing

69. Obedient - acquiescent, amenable, attentive, biddable, complaisant, compliant, controllable, deferential, devoted, docile, docious, duteous, dutiful, faithful, governable, honoring, law-abiding, loyal, obeisant, obliging, observant, pliant, regardful, resigned, respectful, reverential, sheep-like, submissive, subservient, tame, tractable, under control, venerating, well-trained, willing, yes, yielding

70. Obliging - accommodating, agreeable, amiable, cheerful, civil, complaisant, considerate, cooperative, courteous, easy, easy-going, good-humored, good-natured, helpful, hospitable, kind, lenient, mild, polite, willing

71. Optimistic - assured, bright, buoyant, cheerful, cheering, confident, encouraged, expectant, happy, high, hopeful, hoping, idealistic, merry, positive, promising, rose-colored, rosy, sanguine, sunny, trusting, upbeat, Utopian

72. Outgoing - approachable, civil, communicative, cordial, easy, expansive, extrovert, extroverted, friendly, genial, gregarious, informal, kind, open, sociable, sympathetic, unconstrained, unreserved, unrestrained, warm

73. Outspoken - abrupt, artless, blunt, candid, direct, forthright, frank, free, open, plain, plain-spoken, point-blank, round, square, straightforward, strident, talk turkey, unceremonious, unequivocal, unreserved, unreticent, up front, vocal

74. Particular - accurate, appropriate, blow-by-blow, circumstantial, clocklike, detailed, distinct, especial, exact, express, full, individual, intrinsic, itemized, limited, local, meticulous, minute, painstaking, particularized, peculiar, precise, scrupulous, selective, singular, special, thorough, topical

75. Patient - accommodating, calm, composed, easy-going, enduring, even-tempered, forbearing, forgiving, gentle, imperturbable, indulgent, lenient, long-suffering, meek, mild, mild-tempered, persevering, persistent, philosophic, philosophical, quiet, resigned, self-possessed, serene, stoical, submissive, tolerant, tranquil, uncomplaining, understanding, unruffled, untiring

76. Peaceful - all quiet, amicable, at peace, bloodless, calm, collected, composed, constant, easeful, equable, gentle, halcyon, harmonious, irenic, level, mellow, neutral, neutralist, nonbelligerent, nonviolent, pacifistic, peace-loving, peaceable, placatory, placid, quiet, restful, serene, smooth, sociable, steady, still, tranquil, undisturbed, unruffled, untroubled, without hostility

77. Perfectionist - accurate, cautious, conscientious, conscionable, exact, fastidious, fussy, heedful, microscopic, nitpicking, painstaking, particular, persnickety, picky, precise, punctilious, punctual, scrupulous, stickling, strict, thorough

78. Persistent - assiduous, bound, bulldogged, constant, continual, continuous, dogged, endless, enduring, firm, fixed, hang tough, immovable, incessant, indefatigable, insistent, interminable, never-ending, obdurate, obstinate, perpetual, perseverant, persevering, persisting, pertinacious, relentless, repeated, resolute, steadfast, steady, stick-to-itive, sticky, stubborn, tenacious, tireless, unflagging, unrelenting, unremitting, unshakable

79. Persuasive - actuating, alluring, cogent, compelling, conclusive, convictive, convincing, credible, effective, effectual, efficacious, efficient, eloquent, energetic, enticing, forceful, forcible, impelling, impressive, inducing, inspiring, inveigling, logical, luring, moving, plausible, pointed, potent, powerful, seductive, slick, smooth, sound, stimulating, stringent, strong, swaying, telling, touching, unctuous, valid, weighty, wheedling, winning

80. Placid - collected, composed, cool, detached, easy, easygoing, equable, even, even-tempered, gentle, halcyon, hushed, imperturbable, inexcitable, irenic, mild, peaceful, poised, quiet, restful, self-possessed, serene, still, tranquil, unagitated, undisturbed, unexcitable, unflappable, unmoved, unruffled, untroubled

81. Playful - antic, blithe, cheerful, coltish, comical, elvish, flirtatious, frisky, frolicsome, funny, gamesome, gay, go-go, good-natured, happy, hilarious, humorous, impish, jaunty, jesting, jocund, joking, joyous, kittenish, lighthearted, lively, merry, mirthful, mischievous, peppy, pixie, prankish, puckish, roguish, rollicking, snappy, spirited, sportive, sprightly, teasing, tongue-in-cheek, vivacious, waggish, whimsical, zippy

82. Precise - absolute, accurate, actual, categorical, circumscribed, clear-cut, correct, decisive, definite, determinate, explicit, express, fixed, individual, limited, literal, narrow, nice, particular, proper, restricted, right, rigid, rigorous, specific, strict, stringent, unequivocal, very, well-defined

83. Predictable - anticipated, calculable, certain, expected, foreseeable, foreseen, likely, prepared, sure, sure-fire

84. Private - concealed, discreet, isolated, quiet, removed, retired, secluded, secret, separate, sequestered, solitary, withdrawn

85. Realistic - astute, businesslike, commonsense, down-to-earth, earthy, hard, hard-boiled, level-headed, matter-of-fact, practical, pragmatic, pragmatical, prudent, rational, real, reasonable, sane, sensible, shrewd, sober, sound, unfantastic, unidealistic, unromantic, unsentimental, utilitarian

86. Reserved - aloof, backward, bashful, cautious, ceremonious, close, close-mouthed, cold, collected, composed, conventional, cool, demure, diffident, distant, eremitic, formal, gentle, icy, mild, misanthropic, modest, noncommittal, offish, peaceful, placid, prim, quiet, reclusive, restrained, reticent, retiring, secretive, sedate, self-contained, serene, shy, soft-spoken, solitary, standoffish, taciturn, unapproachable, uncommunicative, uncompanionable, undemonstrative, unresponsive, withdrawn

87. Restrained - aseptic, bottled up, chilled, conservative, controlled, cool, corked up, discreet, hip, hog-tied, hung up, iced, in charge, in check, inobtrusive, laid-back, mild, moderate, muted, on leash, plain, quiet, reasonable, reticent, retiring, self-controlled, shrinking, soft, square, steady, subdued, tasteful, temperate, unaffable, undemonstrative, under control, under wraps, unexcessive, unexpansive, unextreme, unobtrusive, uptight, withdrawn

88. Satisfied - at ease, at peace, cheerful, comfortable, complacent, content, glad, gratified, pleased, serene, thankful

89. Self-Starter - aggressive, anxious, ardent, aspiring, avid, ballsy, bent upon, climbing, come on, designing, desirous, determined, driving, eager, eager beaver, earnest, energetic, enterprising, enthusiastic, fireball, goal-oriented, hard ball, high-reaching, hopeful, hungry, industrious, inspired, intent, longing, power-loving, purposeful, pushing, pushy, resourceful, self-starting, sharp, soaring, spark plug, striving, thirsty, vaulting, zealous

90. Serene - at peace, clear, collected, comfortable, composed, content, cool, dispassionate, easy, easygoing, fair, halcyon, imperturbable, laid back, limpid, patient, peaceful, pellucid, phlegmatic, placid, poised, quiescent, quiet, reconciled, resting, satisfied, sedate, self-possessed, smooth, still, stoical, tranquil, undisturbed, unflappable, unruffled, untroubled

91. Sociable - accessible, affable, approachable, close, clubby, companionable, conversable, convivial, cordial, familiar, genial, good-natured, gregarious, intimate, mix, neighborly, outgoing, regular, right neighborly, social, warm, white

92. Soft-Spoken - apprehensive, backward, bashful, biddable, blushing, content, courteous, deferential, demure, diffident, docile, fearful, gentle, hesitant, lowly, manageable, mild, modest, obliging, obsequious, ordinary, polite, quiet, reserved, respectful, retiring, reverential, sedate, self-conscious, self-effacing, servile, sheepish, shy, simple, standoffish, submissive, subservient, supplicatory, tentative, timid, timorous, tractable, unambitious, unobtrusive, unostentatious, unpretentious, withdrawn

93. Strong-Minded - bullheaded, contrary, determined, foolhardy, froward, hard core, hard shell, hard-nosed, heedless, imprudent, impulsive, intractable, locked in, mule, mulish, murder, obstinate, perverse, pig-headed, rash, reckless, refractory, self-willed, uncontrollable, ungovernable, unruly, unyielding, willful

94. Structured - all together, analytical, businesslike, careful, deliberate, disciplined, efficient, exact, fixed, framed, grooved, logical, methodic, methodized, meticulous, neat, ordered, orderly, painstaking, planned, precise, regular, scrupulous, set up, systematic, tidy, together, well-regulated

95. Stubborn - adamant, balky, bull-headed, cantankerous, contumacious, cussed, determined, dogged, firm, fixed, hard-headed, headstrong, inexorable, inflexible, insubordinate, intractable, mulish, obdurate, opinionated, ornery, persevering, persistent, pertinacious, perverse, pig-headed, rebellious, recalcitrant, refractory, relentless, rigid, self-willed, single-minded, steadfast, stiff-necked, tenacious, tough, unbending, unmanageable, unreasonable, unshakable, untoward, unyielding, willful

96. Sympathetic - affectionate, all heart, appreciating, benign, benignant, bleeding heart, caring, commiserating, compassionate, comprehending, concerned, condoling, considerate, interested, kind, kind-hearted, kindly, loving, old softie, pitying, responsive, sensitive, soft-hearted, supportive, sympathizing, tender, thoughtful, understanding, vicarious, warm, warm-hearted

97. Systematic - analytical, arranged, businesslike, complete, efficient, logical, methodic, methodical, ordered, organized, out-and-out, precise, regular, standardized, systematized, thoroughgoing, well-ordered

98. Tactful - adroit, aware, careful, cautious, civil, considerate, courteous, deft, delicate, diplomatic, discreet, gentle, judicious, observant, perceptive, poised, polished, polite, politic, prudent, sensitive, skilled, skillful, statesmanlike, suave, subtle, sympathetic, tactical, understanding, urbane, wise

99. Talkative - articulate, big-mouthed, chattering, chatty, effusive, eloquent, fluent, gabbling, gabby, garrulous, gassy, glib, gossipy, long-winded, loose-lipped, loquacious, loudmouth, mouthy, multiloquent, prolix, rattling, slick, smooth, talky, verbal, verbose, vocal, voluble, windy, wordy, yacky

100. Tenacious - adamant, bent on, bound, bulldogged, clinging, coherent, cohesive, determined, dogged, fast, firm, forceful, inflexible, intransigent, iron, mean business, mulish, obdurate, obstinate, persevering, persistent, persisting, pertinacious, possessive, purposeful, relentless, resolute, retentive, set, solid, spunky, stalwart, staunch, steadfast, stout, strong-willed, stubborn, sturdy, sure, tight, tough, true, unforgetful, unshakable, unswerving, unyielding

101. Thorough - absolute, all-embracing, all-inclusive, all-out, assiduous, blow-by-blow, careful, circumstantial, clocklike, complete, comprehensive, conscientious, detailed, efficient, exact, full, full-dress, in-depth, intensive, itemized, meticulous, minute, painstaking, particular, particularized, plenty, royal, scrupulous, slam bang, sweeping, thoroughgoing, tough, whole-hog

102. Tolerant - advanced, benevolent, big, broad, broad-minded, catholic, charitable, clement, complaisant, condoning, easy on, easy with, easy-going, excusing, fair, forbearing, forgiving, humane, indulgent, kind-hearted, lax, lenient, liberal, long-suffering, magnanimous, merciful, patient, permissive, progressive, radical, receptive, soft, soft shell, sophisticated, sympathetic, understanding, unprejudiced, wide

103. Traditional - acceptable, accustomed, acknowledged, ancestral, classic, classical, common, conventional, customary, doctrinal, established, fixed, folk, habitual, historic, immemorial, long-established, old, oral, popular, prescribed, regular, rooted, sanctioned, time-honored, transmitted, universal, unwritten, widely used, widespread

104. Willing - accommodating, active, amenable, cheerful, compliant, consenting, content, deliberate, desirous, disposed, eager, energetic, enthusiastic, fair, favorable, feeling, forward, game, happy, in favor, inclined, intentional, like, minded, obedient, on, pleased, predisposed, prepared, prompt, prone, ready, reliable, responsible, tractable, unasked, unbidden, unforced, voluntary, well-disposed, willful, witting, zealous

Thesaurus

Understanding the Extreme Lion

Your responses indicate that your style is that of an "extreme" lion, suggesting you display the characteristics of the lion style very intensely.

You are very much an extrovert--confident and self-assured-- enjoying the outer world of activities and being energized in the presence of others. When it comes to getting things done, however, you are also more task-oriented than people-oriented. Your extreme lion qualities make you well suited for leadership as you are likely to be highly assertive, decisive, and outspoken in your relationships with others. Your ability to think strategically and independently gives you an advantage in achieving the results that are important to you, and you are more than willing to be accountable for those results.

When others interact with you, they will likely notice that you look people in the eye and move quickly and with purpose. Your speaking style is fast paced and forceful, and you tend to tell people what you think very directly. You may sometimes enjoy working for fun, but in your working mode, you prefer to work quickly to get the task or project finished without wasting time. Because you have a bias towards getting right to the "bottom line," you may have more difficulty than some when required to focus for long periods of time. In competitive situations, you hate to lose.

Extreme lions can find it a struggle to adapt to styles that are different from their own. When extreme lions are stressed, their characteristic behaviors can lead to the perception that they are dictating to others rather than leading. Their directness and "get-it-done" attitude can turn into impatience or aggressiveness that can cause others to feel intimidated or "bossed around."

As an extreme lion, you need to be on guard for those situations in which your "inner lion's" desire to achieve and get results shows up as intolerance of others' ideas and approaches. You also run the risk of appearing short-tempered and egotistical rather than direct, assertive, and self-confident.

The Extreme Lion's Strengths

The following qualities and characteristics are strengths of the lion style you have in abundance. These can be emphasized and leveraged to advantage in a variety of situations and relationships.

- **Assertiveness** – Willing to speak up, express your wishes clearly, and state what you want without being intimidated by others.
- **Results-Oriented** – Focusing on clear goals and standards for achievement; seeking the most direct path to tangible payoffs for any endeavor; impatient with fuzzy or unclear objectives; not liking to waste time on efforts that seem less likely to produce concrete results.
- **Directness** – Ability to get straight to the point, say what you mean, and be understood clearly.
- **Forcefulness** – Willingness to take responsibility for your actions, stand up for what you believe is right, and accept the consequences when you make a mistake.
- **Ambition** – Being strongly goal oriented and self-directed, willing to take action to achieve your goals.
- **Confidence** – Having strong faith in yourself and your abilities; belief in your own self-worth.
- **Courage** – Willing to step up to difficult challenges without undue fear of the consequences; able to confront difficult situations head on; able to move ahead in the face of uncertainty.
- **Self-Assuredness** – Having a sense of what is right for yourself and others; a willingness to act in an even-handed way without personal bias or favoritism.

The Extreme Lion's Interpersonal Challenges

As often the case, great strengths can also be manifested as potential weaknesses. The following are some common characteristics observed in extreme lions when they are at their least effective:

- **Aggressive** – Quick to push back or go on the attack; seen as domineering.
- **Impatient** – Finding it challenging to focus and concentrate for long periods of time.
- **Controlling** – Acting to determine what will happen and how things are done; limiting others' choices; manipulating situations to achieve their own ends at the expense of others' wishes and desires.
- **Argumentative** – Tendency to be one-sided; close-minded to others' viewpoints or opinions; pushing too hard to persuade others of the rightness of their position rather than listening to other perspectives.
- **Poor Listening** – tendency to want to talk rather than hear what others are saying; missing the meaning or intent of others' communication; tendency to interrupt when others are trying to speak.
- **Short-Tempered** – Being impatient, curt, irritable with others; easily losing one's composure when frustrated or unable to achieve a desired objective or goal; lacking self-control in trying situations.
- **Intimidating** – causing others to feel a lack of confidence in expressing themselves or asking for what they want; lowering others' self-esteem and sense of self-worth.
- **Poor Adaptability** – Little or no tolerance for others' styles; lacking the will or ability to   modify their own style to accommodate the needs and preferences of others, especially those with more introverted or people-oriented styles.

Increasing Interpersonal Effectiveness for Extreme Lions

Here are some suggestions to leverage your strengths and avoid potential interpersonal pitfalls in common work situations such as meetings, team interactions, supervising others, and giving feedback.

◎ Develop good listening skills

- ⬛ Pay conscious attention when others are speaking, maintaining eye contact and responding nonverbally. (Nodding, etc.)
- ⬛ Use paraphrases to show you understand what the person has said. ("So, what you are saying is . . .")
- ⬛ Show empathy for feelings that others express. ("I understand why that would have been a frustrating situation for you.")

◎ Demonstrate openness to others' ideas and points of view.

- ⬛ Hold off on criticism until you have heard the entire viewpoint.
- ⬛ Offer a positive statement or constructive addition to the idea on the table.
- ⬛ Avoid appearing to "shoot down" ideas and instead, ask questions to clarify what the person means.
- ⬛ Look for an aspect or part of the opinion that you can agree with and incorporate it into your perspective.
- ⬛ If you don't agree with something, say so in a direct way, focusing on facts and issues rather than implying a criticism of the person holding the opinion.

◎ Work towards a participative approach to making decisions and choosing actions.

- ⬛ Rather than making decisions yourself, invite others to offer their opinions and ideas.
- ⬛ When decisions are on the table, consciously maintain an open mind and invite others to share options and perspectives.
- ⬛ Set aside your own preferences, and listen first for the pros and cons of alternative choices.

- Remember to give others a turn at having their preferences put first.

Practice adaptability

- Pay conscious attention to how others communicate – whether they are slower, more deliberate speakers, more expressive of their emotions, or want to discuss more details than you would prefer.
- Make a deliberate effort to show interest, patience, and responsiveness.
- Curb impulses to interrupt, close the conversation, or hurry the speaker to "get to the point."
- Remind yourself that each style has its own strengths and value.

When interacting with doves in particular, you will be more effective if you:

- Make a special effort to avoid intimidating behaviors that can cause them to withdraw or shut down communication.
- Ask for their input and listen to their ideas and opinions.
- Take a cooperative rather than confrontational approach to resolving differences.
- Demonstrate support for their interests and feelings.

Understanding the Strong Lion

Your responses indicate you are a strong lion. As an extrovert, you like to participate in activities that include other people, though in your work mode you tend to be more task-oriented than people-oriented. Your lion qualities of courage, decisiveness, and confidence make you a natural leader, and your ability to think strategically and independently gives you an advantage in achieving the results that are important to you. Although you are competitive and hate to lose, you have a sense of fairness that encourages playing by the rules and being even handed when you make judgments and decisions. You are willing to take risks to achieve a goal and are also willing to be accountable for the results and consequences of your actions and decisions.

The characteristics people notice when they interact with you include your direct eye contact and tendency to speak quickly and forcefully. You are likely to be very direct in stating what you think and want, and you move at a fast, purposeful pace. Although you often enjoy having fun when working, you prefer to work quickly and efficiently to get the task or project finished without wasting time. Because you have a bias towards getting right to the "bottom line," you may have more difficulty than some when required to focus for long periods of time. In competitive situations, you dislike losing.

When strong lions are stressed, their actions and behaviors can appear dictatorial and intimidating, causing others to perceive the lion style as being bossy rather than leading in a positive way.

To optimize your effectiveness, you need to temper your "inner lion's" desire to achieve and get results with tolerance for others' ideas and preferred ways of getting things done. Without this self-awareness, a strong lion runs the risk of appearing to be short-tempered, impatient, and egotistical when rather than direct, assertive, and self-confident. You may have a tendency to ignore or deny feelings--your own as well as those of others. This can cause tension in situations in which feelings need to be discussed and managed.

The Strong Lion's Strengths

The following qualities and characteristics are strengths of the lion style that can be leveraged to advantage in a variety of situations and relationships.

- **Assertiveness** – Willing to speak up, express your wishes clearly, and state what you want without being intimidated by others.
- **Results-Oriented** – Focusing on clear goals and standards for achievement; seeking the most direct path to tangible payoffs for any endeavor; impatient with fuzzy or unclear objectives; not liking to waste time on efforts that seem less likely to produce concrete results.
- **Directness** – Ability to get straight to the point, say what you mean, and be understood clearly.
- **Forcefulness** – Willingness to take responsibility for your actions, stand up for what you believe is right, and accept the consequences when you make a mistake.
- **Ambition** – Being strongly goal oriented and self-directed, willing to take action to achieve your goals.
- **Confidence** – Having strong faith in yourself and your abilities; belief in your own self-worth.
- **Courage** – Willing to step up to difficult challenges without undue fear of the consequences; able to confront difficult situations head on; able to move ahead in the face of uncertainty.
- **Self-Assuredness** – Having a sense of what is right for you and others; a willingness to act in an even-handed way without personal bias or favoritism.

The Strong Lion's Interpersonal Challenges

As is often the case, our strengths can be connected to potential weaknesses. The following are some common characteristics observed in lions when they are not at their best.

- **Aggressive** – Quick to push back or go on the attack; seen as domineering.
- **Impatient** – Finding it challenging to focus and concentrate for long periods of time.
- **Controlling** – Acting to determine what will happen and how things are done; limiting others' choices; manipulating situations to achieve their own ends at the expense of others' wishes and desires.
- **Argumentative** – Tendency to be one-sided; close-minded to others' viewpoints or opinions; pushing too hard to persuade others of the rightness of their position rather than listening to other perspectives.
- **Poor Listening** – Wanting to talk rather than hear what others are saying; missing the meaning or intent of others' communication; tendency to interrupt when others are trying to speak.
- **Short-Tempered** – Being impatient, curt, and irritable with others; easily losing one's composure when frustrated or unable to achieve a desired objective or goal; lacking self-control in trying situations.
- **Intimidating** – causing others to feel a lack of confidence in expressing themselves or asking for what they want; lowering others' self-esteem and sense of self-worth.
- **Intolerant** – Unwilling to give others time to process information or express their ideas; tendency to cut off discussions or deliberations; close minded.

Increasing Interpersonal Effectiveness for Strong Lions

Here are some suggestions to leverage your strengths and avoid potential interpersonal pitfalls in common work situations such as meetings, team interactions, supervising others, and giving feedback.

◉ Develop good listening skills

- ▸ Pay conscious attention when others are speaking, maintaining eye contact and responding nonverbally. (Nodding, etc.)
- ▸ Use paraphrases to show you understand what the person has said. ("So, what you are saying is . . .")
- ▸ Show empathy for feelings that are expressed. ("I understand why that would have been a frustrating situation for you.")

◉ Demonstrate openness to others' ideas and points of view.

- ▸ Hold off on criticism until you have heard the entire viewpoint.
- ▸ Offer a positive statement or constructive addition to the idea on the table.
- ▸ Avoid appearing to "shoot down" an idea, and instead, ask questions to clarify what the person means.
- ▸ Look for an aspect or part of the opinion that you can agree with and incorporate it into your perspective.
- ▸ If you don't agree with something, say so in a direct way, focusing on facts and issues rather than implying a criticism of the person holding the opinion.

◉ Practice a participative approach to making decisions and choosing actions.

- ▸ Rather than making decisions yourself, invite others to offer their opinions and ideas.
- ▸ When decisions are on the table, consciously maintain an open mind and invite others to share options and perspectives.
- ▸ Set aside your own preferences, and listen first for the pros and cons of alternative choices.

▣ Remember to give others a turn at having their preferences put first.

◉ Cultivate empathy and understanding of what others are feeling and experiencing.

▣ Pay attention to nonverbal expressions of emotion, including facial expression, tone of voice, and physical tension.

▣ Listen for language that indicates emotional tension, such as "this situation is frustrating," or "I feel my opinions are being ignored."

▣ Ask questions to understand what others are feeling.

▣ Express your understanding and concern with statements such as, "I can see that this situation is upsetting for you," or "having your opinions ignored must be frustrating for you."

Understanding the Extreme Peacock

Your responses indicate that your style is that of an "extreme" peacock, suggesting that you display the characteristics of the peacock style very intensely. You are a strong extrovert, meaning you enjoy activities in the outer world and are energized by being with other people. In your working mode, you are people-oriented and often play the role of the "ring leader," motivating and inspiring others. In your interactions with others, you are highly sociable, lively, and friendly, infusing humor, enthusiasm, and energy into your relationships. Since peacocks tend to be creative and visionary, you are able to generate a lot of great ideas, and your skill at persuasion will help you gain others' support. This ability to enlist others in achieving your goals is one of your greatest strengths, and your self-confidence and talent for influencing others contribute to your effectiveness when making public presentations.

When others interact with you, they will likely notice that you speak quickly, expressively, and animatedly, and your co-workers probably know you as someone who works quickly and with high energy and enthusiasm. Because you expend so much energy when you are at a high point, you may find that you can also "crash" and experience noticeable highs and lows in your mood.

Extreme peacocks can face challenges in their work and relationships with others, especially when they are not emphasizing the best, most positive elements of their style.

When extreme peacocks are stressed, they express their feelings with great intensity, sometimes acting out towards others in a way that creates tension and hurts relationships. As much as they love the excitement of generating new ideas and starting fresh projects, extreme peacocks often find it difficult to finish as many projects as they start. Because they hate getting bogged down in details, they can end up being inattentive to those that matter, resulting in a perception that they are careless, irresponsible, or superficial.

Too much enthusiasm can be a problem for extreme peacocks as well, leading to a tendency to oversell themselves or an idea, and creating the impression of their being impulsive or frivolous. In general, extreme peacocks run the risk of overwhelming those with less assertive styles. The result is that others may hold back or withdraw from interactions in which they feel they have no "space" to be heard or to express themselves.

The Extreme Peacock's Strengths

The following qualities and characteristics are strengths of the peacock style you have in abundance that can be emphasized and leveraged to advantage in a variety of situations and relationships.

- **Gregarious** – Sociable, outgoing; finding it easy to strike up conversations and develop relationships and networks; conversing confidently with a wide variety of people, including strangers in new settings; can be the "life of the party," the center of attention, and the leader of social activities.
- **Energetic** – Being action oriented and forceful in tackling tasks; taking the initiative to bring about an effect or reach a goal.
- **Influential** – Ability to exert an effect on others without the need for power or authority; ability to gain support and cooperation from others; convincing, able to induce others to change their views or take actions they might not have taken otherwise.
- **Optimistic** – Expecting positive outcomes, seeing the bright side of life, focusing on the future rather than the past, seeing possibilities in situations rather than dwelling on the problems.
- **Visionary** – Being able to imagine the future in a way that inspires others; articulating compelling goals that are motivating for individuals and groups; being innovative in thinking about possibilities others may miss.
- **Innovative** – Embracing and driving change rather than resisting it.
- **Humorous** – Able to appreciate the lighter side of life; enjoying laughter and being comfortable with people who like to joke or tease; able to use humor to diffuse tension or lift others' spirits.
- **Enthusiastic** – Responding positively to people or situations; displaying strong support for ideas and proposals that can help generate support in others; maintaining positive emotions that can help motivate others.

The Extreme Peacock's Interpersonal Challenges

As is often the case, great strengths can be connected to potential weaknesses. The following are some common characteristics observed in peacocks when they are at their least effective.

- **Verbose** – Dominating the conversation, taking too long to get to the point, not considering others' interests and preferences.
- **Irresponsible** – Evading accountability for tasks or accepting the consequences of their actions; failing to anticipate and plan for contingencies or problems; letting others down by lack of foresight; failing to share in creating solutions for problems.
- **Impulsive** – Acting too quickly without considering the potential consequences, sometimes resulting in unnecessary problems and wasted time and effort.
- **Hyper** – Overactive and overly expressive of feelings; making others uncomfortable with high levels of unfocused activity.
- **Manipulative** – Using skills of persuasion and influence to convince others to take action or make decisions for their own interests rather than those of others.
- **Flighty** – Having little sense of purpose or seriousness, changeable and unreliable, lacking focus.
- **Overselling** – Unrealistic view of reality; making promises they can't keep; failing to take into account both the pros and cons of a decision or action.
- **Poor Adaptability** – Ignoring others' style preferences and needs, especially those who are less assertive, resulting in "shutting down" their communication and short-circuiting one-on-one or group interactions.

Increasing Interpersonal Effectiveness for Extreme Peacocks

Here are some suggestions to leverage your strengths and avoid potential interpersonal pitfalls in common work situations such as meetings, team interactions, supervising others, and giving feedback.

◎ Develop good listening skills

- ➡ Focus on attending to others in one-on-one or group situations; watch for indicators that others want to speak, and make sure you are yielding the floor to let someone else speak rather than taking up too much of the "conversational space."
- ➡ When others are speaking, show you are attentive by maintaining eye contact and responding nonverbally. (Nodding, etc.)
- ➡ Use paraphrases to demonstrate you understand what the person has said. ("So, what you are saying is . . .")
- ➡ Show empathy for feelings others express. ("I understand why that would have been a frustrating situation for you.")

◎ Show accountability and reliability in team and work group efforts.

- ➡ Set realistic, achievable goals, and think through the plan for how you will achieve them.
- ➡ Avoid over promising or over selling. Commit to a few things you can accomplish, and follow through.
- ➡ Involve others in planning and considering possible contingencies; make sure you have a back-up plan for potential problems.

◎ Demonstrate positive intentions and concern for others' interests.

- ➡ Look for "win-win" decisions and choices that focus on optimizing benefits for as many people as possible rather than for you alone or you and your group.

- When seeking to persuade or influence others, determine what their interests and concerns are rather than focusing exclusively on your own.
- Be open about stating what your interests are, and discuss candidly how they are or are not aligned with those of the other people involved.
- Listen to other points of view and perspectives, and look for solutions and decisions that accommodate as many different perspectives as possible.
- Be willing to put others' interests ahead of your own in situations in which you can be accommodating without jeopardizing a critical value or you can "live with" a compromise solution.

Practice adaptability

- Pay conscious attention to how others communicate, whether they are slower, more deliberate speakers, less assertive about stating what they are feeling or what they need, or more interested in discussing details than you are.
- Make a deliberate effort to be patient, show interest, and ask questions to help you better understand their thinking, interests, and feelings.
- Curb impulses to interrupt or guess what the other person is going to say.
- Remind yourself that each style has its own strengths and value.

When interacting with turtles in particular, you will be more effective if you:

- Make a special effort to pay attention to details and focus on being well organized when you are responsible for leading meetings, projects, or other team efforts.
- Support your ideas and opinions with facts and evidence; be careful not to overstate your case or over sell your point of view.
- If presenting to an audience that includes a significant number of turtles, use graphic representations of data such as charts and graphs.
- Make time for processing information and weighing options; don't try to rush to a quick decision.
- Ask for their help in analyzing information, generating options and back-up plans, and identifying potential trouble spots or contingencies.

Understanding the Strong Peacock

Your responses indicate that your style is that of strong peacock. You are an extrovert--outgoing and people-oriented--enjoying activities that involve others. You are usually lively and friendly in work and social situations and are likely known for bringing humor, enthusiasm, and energy into your relationships. Since peacocks tend to be creative and visionary, you are often able to generate new ideas, and your skill at influencing others helps you gain support and cooperation for getting things done. This ability to enlist others in achieving your goals is one of your greatest strengths, and your self-confidence and talent for motivating and inspiring others contribute to your effectiveness in making public presentations.

When others interact with you, they will likely notice that you speak expressively and animatedly, and your co-workers probably know you as someone who works quickly and with high energy and enthusiasm. You may experience noticeable highs and lows in mood but are generally optimistic and self-confident--qualities that help you adapt well to change.

Peacocks can face challenges when they are not emphasizing the best, most positive elements of their style. When they are stressed, peacocks may express their feelings intensely, in a way that creates tension and may harm relationships. They can also find it difficult to finish as many projects as they start and sometimes overlook details others see as important. When this happens, peacocks can be perceived as careless, irresponsible, or superficial. Too much enthusiasm can be a problem when it leads to "over selling" themselves or an idea, creating the impression of being impulsive or frivolous.

In general, peacocks can run the risk of overwhelming those with less assertive styles, causing them to hold back or withdraw from interactions in which they feel they have no "space" to express themselves.

The Peacock's Strengths

The following qualities and characteristics are strengths of the peacock style that can be emphasized and leveraged for positive results in a variety of situations and relationships.

- **Gregarious** – Sociable, outgoing; finding it easy to strike up conversations and develop relationships and networks; conversing confidently with a wide variety of people, including strangers in new settings; can be the "life of the party," the center of attention, and a leader of social activities.
- **Energetic** – Being action oriented and forceful in tackling tasks; taking the initiative to bring about an effect or reach a goal.
- **Influential** – Ability to exert an effect on others without the need for power or authority; ability to gain support and cooperation from others; convincing, able to induce others to change their views or take actions they might not have taken otherwise.
- **Optimistic** – Expecting positive outcomes, seeing the bright side of life, focusing on the future rather than the past, seeing possibilities in situations rather than dwelling on the problems.
- **Visionary** – Being able to imagine the future in a way that inspires others; articulating compelling goals that are motivating for individuals and groups; being innovative in thinking about possibilities others may miss.
- **Innovative** – Embracing and driving change rather than resisting it.
- **Humorous** – Able to appreciate the lighter side of life; enjoying laughter and being comfortable with people who like to joke or tease; able to use humor to diffuse tension or lift others' spirits.
- **Enthusiastic** – Responding positively to people or situations; displaying strong support for ideas and proposals that can help generate support in others; maintaining positive emotions that can help motivate others.

The Peacock's Interpersonal Challenges

As is often the case, great strengths can lead to potential weaknesses. The following are some common characteristics observed in peacocks when they are at their least effective.

- **Verbose** – Dominating the conversation, taking too long to get to the point, not considering others' interests and preferences.
- **Irresponsible** – Evading accountability for tasks or accepting the consequences of their actions; failing to anticipate and plan for contingencies or problems; letting others down by lack of foresight; failing to share in creating solutions for problems.
- **Impulsive** – Acting too quickly without considering the potential consequences, sometimes resulting in unnecessary problems and wasted time and effort.
- **Hyper** – Overactive and over expressive of feelings; making others uncomfortable with high levels of unfocused activity.
- **Manipulative** – Using skills of persuasion and influence to convince others to take action or make decisions for their own interests rather than those of others.
- **Flighty** – Having little sense of purpose or seriousness, changeable and unreliable, lacking focus.
- **Overselling** – Unrealistic view of reality; making promises they can't keep; failing to take into account both the pros and cons of a decision or action.
- **Superficial** – Shallow thinking focused on ideas and goals others see as unimportant; lacking seriousness or depth; little interest in thinking about and discussing more complex or demanding problems and issues.

Increasing Interpersonal Effectiveness for Strong Peacocks

Here are some suggestions for leveraging your strengths and avoiding potential interpersonal pitfalls in common work situations such as meetings, team interactions, supervising others, and giving feedback.

◉ Develop good listening skills

- ▣ Focus on attending to others in one-on-one or group situations; watch for indicators that others want to speak, and make sure you yield the floor to let someone else speak rather than taking up too much of the "conversational space."
- ▣ When others are speaking, show you are attentive by maintaining eye contact and responding nonverbally. (Nodding, etc.)
- ▣ Use paraphrases to demonstrate your grasp of the other person's meaning. ("So, what you are saying is . . .")
- ▣ Show empathy for others' feelings by articulating your understanding and concern. ("I understand why that would have been a frustrating situation for you.")

◉ Demonstrate accountability and reliability in team and work group efforts.

- ▣ Set realistic, achievable goals, and think through the plan for how you will achieve them.
- ▣ Avoid over promising or over selling. Commit to a few things you can accomplish, and follow through.
- ▣ Involve others in planning and considering possible contingencies; make sure you have a back-up plan for potential problems.

◉ Show your positive intentions and concern for others' interests.

- ▣ Look for "win-win" decisions and choices that focus on optimizing benefits for as many people as possible rather than you alone or you and your group.

- When seeking to persuade or influence others, determine what their interests and concerns are rather than focusing exclusively on your own.
- Be open about stating what your interests are, and discuss candidly how they are or are not aligned with those of the other people involved.
- Listen to other points of view and perspectives, and look for solutions and decisions that accommodate as many different perspectives as possible.
- Be willing to put others' interests ahead of your own in situations in which you can be accommodating without jeopardizing a critical value or you can "live with" a compromise solution.

Raise your standards of accuracy and attention to detail.

- Think through the requirements for plans and goals, and identify the key details that must be considered to achieve success.
- Allow time to check your work for factual accuracy; use an editor if necessary to correct errors.
- et input and feedback from others who have knowledge and expertise in the subject at hand.
- When presenting ideas and plans to gain support from others, include back-up data and materials such as charts and graphs rather than relying only on your powers of personal persuasion.

Understanding the Extreme Dove

Your responses indicate that your style is that of an "extreme" dove, suggesting that you display the characteristics of the dove style very intensely.

You are very much an introvert, meaning that you are energized by your inner world of ideas and impressions, and may often need to spend time alone to think things through and "recharge" your energy. On the other hand, you are people-oriented more than task-oriented in your working mode. In your relationships with others, you are caring and unselfish, known for nurturing and helping others meet their needs.

Because you are so group-oriented, others see you as a team player, and your cooperative and supportive approach to getting things done makes you an excellent member of a team or task group. You are generally able to maintain self-control and stability even in stressful conditions, and your diplomatic skills help you avoid conflict, which you dislike intensely. In social situations, you are easygoing, relaxed, and likeable, making others feel comfortable and at ease.

When others interact with you, they notice that you are sensitive to others' feelings, and that you speak at an even pace, in softer tones, making frequent eye contact. You don't like to draw attention to yourself, and in group settings, you will listen more than you talk. People who work or socialize with you on a regular basis feel comfortable that you are predictable and reliable, and they will count on you to be patient and steady in most situations.

When extreme doves are stressed, they may tend to withdraw and are prone to appear stubborn and even whiney rather than patient and steady. Extreme doves face challenges because they find it difficult to be assertive, and often are intimidated in situations that may involve friction or the threat of conflict. As a result, they may find their needs are not met and their wishes and opinions get ignored. When this happens, extreme doves may fall into the trap of feeling like martyrs or become too dependent on others to protect their interests. Because of the strong desire to avoid conflict, extreme doves may end up accepting mediocre work. They may avoid decision making, even in situations in which others assume it is their responsibility to set standards and take a leadership role in a decision.

Your Score Explained

Extreme doves also may find it difficult to complete tasks in a timely manner and in a way that produces results others expect. Contributing factors include unwillingness to exercise sufficient authority in situations in which they are accountable for others' results, avoiding or procrastinating on making decisions, missing deadlines, procrastinating on giving feedback, and being overly lenient when firmness is required.

The Extreme Dove's Strengths

The following qualities and characteristics are strengths of the dove style you have in abundance that can be emphasized and leveraged to advantage in a variety of situations and relationships.

- **Contemplative** – Being thoughtful, calm, and relaxed; thinking things through rather than rushing to conclusions.
- **Group-Oriented** – Work well with groups and teams to achieve goals; help facilitate teamwork while accomplishing goals and making decisions; willing to recognize and give credit to group efforts rather than seeking individual recognition.
- **Cooperative** – Willing to seek consensus and "win-win" solutions rather than competing to serve their own interests or trying to persuade others to give up theirs; willing to share resources to achieve a common goal.
- **Stable** – Maintaining an "even keel" of emotions and manner; avoiding extremes in moods; being reliably steady in responses to most situations, even those that may be stressful or unpleasant.
- **Patient** – Remaining calm and accepting of others' flaws or failings; allowing time for others to complete their thoughts and present ideas in their own way; maintaining an even emotional state in situations others might find frustrating or exasperating.
- **Unselfish** – Supportive of others' needs; putting others' concerns and interests before their own; freely sharing resources, credit, and recognition with others rather than seeking their own advancement.
- **Nurturing** – Offering support and help to others, especially those who are new, inexperienced, or struggling to learn and grow.
- **Consistent** – Being reliable in how they react and respond to other people; following through on promises and commitments.

The Extreme Dove's Interpersonal Challenges

As is often the case, great strengths can also be manifested as potential weaknesses. The following are some common characteristics observed in extreme doves when they are at their least effective:

- **Easily Intimidated** – Responding to friction, conflict, or aggression with meekness or compliance, sometimes to their own disadvantage; failing to speak up for their own interests or the interests of others; lack of confidence in the face of others' assertiveness, leading to loss of self-esteem.

- **Procrastination** – Putting off tasks that need to be done; finding excuses to avoid taking action; delaying responses to situations that require more immediate and decisive action.

- **Dependency** – Over reliance on others' approval or permission rather than acting on their own to get something done; relying on someone else's authority rather than taking responsibility or accountability for decisions or actions; consistently letting others take the lead rather than stepping forward to take initiative when something needs to be done.

- **Being a Martyr** – Allowing others to take advantage of them rather than asserting their own interests; feeling put upon or abused by others even though they have not clearly asked for help; resenting others for unfair treatment despite the fact that they may be unaware of what doves want.

- **Being Too Lenient** – Failing to exert authority in situations in which it is their responsibility to set standards or provide discipline; avoiding action to correct behaviors of others that may be disruptive or undermining the quality or results of the group; avoiding giving feedback or input that would help bring about improvements due to shyness or fear of conflict.

- **Avoiding Engagement** – Pulling back physically from uncomfortable social situations or situations in which there is conflict or a threat of friction with others; remaining silent and unresponsive in certain situations.

- **Being Too Sensitive** – Overreacting to perceived slights; attaching negative meanings to situations or statements when there are no grounds for the negative interpretation; having their feelings easily hurt by small mistakes or innocent remarks.

- **Poor Adaptability** – Finding it difficult to adjust to others' styles, especially those whose styles are strongly assertive and task related; responding by retreating from the interaction or passively resisting instead of being more direct and forthright in communicating.

Increasing Interpersonal Effectiveness for Extreme Doves

Here are some suggestions to leverage your strengths and avoid potential interpersonal pitfalls in common work situations such as meetings, team interactions, supervising others, and giving feedback.

◎ Cultivate decision making skills

- ▷ Whether you are in a team or leadership position, consciously review and identify your own information, experience, and opinions, and be ready to state them clearly and unambiguously as part of a decision discussion.
- ▷ When it is your responsibility to make a decision, set a deadline for announcing your choice and prepare a clear statement of the decision and the rationale for it; tell others when to expect your announcement and stick to it.
- ▷ If you are unsure about how to make good decisions in complex situations, develop your knowledge and skills by reading articles or books or attending a workshop or seminar. Learn a process for identifying and choosing among options.

◎ Develop independence in thinking and acting

- ▷ Analyze situations in your work and life where you have waited for someone else to take the lead and see what those situations have in common. Ask yourself:
  - Did you lack information or experience that would have helped you take independent action?
  - Were you uncertain of whether you had the authority or right to take action on your own?
  - Did you feel it was too risky to take independent action for which there could possibly be negative consequences?
  - Did you simply lack confidence in your own ability to make a good decision about which action to take?
- ▷ Once you have identified potential issues that keep you from acting independently, set a goal for taking independent action in at least

two or three situations in which you might otherwise feel dependent on others. Make sure you:

- Gather information you need to make a decision or take action.
- Clarify that you have the authority to act independently if you need to.
- Reduce the risks of negative consequences by planning ahead for responding to contingencies.

➡ Practice making independent decisions and taking actions in non-threatening situations at first, and share your results with a friend, manager, or mentor who can help you recognize the benefits and good results of your independence.

◎ Overcome tendency to be too sensitive

➡ Manage your self-talk to give yourself positive messages about others' intentions and the meaning of their remarks or actions.

➡ If you find yourself reacting to a remark or behavior defensively or with hurt feelings, stop and analyze the situation and context. Consider possible alternative explanations for the remark.

➡ If you feel you have been slighted or treated unfairly, think through the specifics of what has happened, and then plan a conversation with the person or people involved.

- In an unemotional, calm manner, describe your feelings without attributing motives or attitudes to the other person.
- Ask the person to respond with his or her interpretation of the situation. Listen attentively without interrupting.
- If it appears that there is indeed a problem, ask for help in avoiding the problem in the future or correcting the situation.
- Agree on a possible solution.

◎ Practice adaptability to other styles.

➡ If you are interacting with others who have more assertive styles, make a deliberate effort to speak up and express your own interests and opinions.

➡ Curb your impulse to withdraw, either physically or mentally, and stay engaged in the conversation; wait for an opening, and then offer your input.

➡ Remind yourself that each style has its own strengths and value.

☺ When interacting with lions, in particular, you will be more effective if you:

- ▶ Be prepared to present your ideas succinctly.
- ▶ Ask explicitly for time to offer your opinions and ideas if you feel you are being intimidated or overwhelmed.
- ▶ Use your diplomatic skills to establish a cooperative rather than adversarial atmosphere.
- ▶ Ask questions to clarify the lion's objectives and intentions, and then take the opportunity to respond to the answers.
- ▶ If there is a conflict or disagreement, engage in a discussion to identify common understanding of the facts and mutually agreed upon solutions rather than withdrawing from the conversation.

Understanding the Strong Dove

Your responses indicate that your style is that of a strong dove.

You are more of an introvert than an extrovert, meaning you often attend to your inner world of ideas and impressions, and may sometimes need time alone to think things through and "recharge" your energy. In your work mode, however, you are people-oriented more than task-oriented and like to support and nurture others.

You are most likely a very effective team player, taking a cooperative and supportive approach to get things done. In stressful conditions, you are good at maintaining self-control and stability rather than giving in to your emotions. You are often able to exercise natural diplomatic skills to help avoid conflict and friction, which often make you uncomfortable. In social situations, you are usually easygoing, relaxed, and likeable, making others feel comfortable and at ease.

When others interact with you, they notice that you are sensitive to others' feelings, and you generally speak at an even pace, in softer tones, making frequent eye contact. You typically avoid drawing attention to yourself in group settings, and tend to listen more than you talk. Most of the time, people find you predictable across a variety of situations, creating a sense of steadiness and reliability they can count on.

When doves are not at their best, they face challenges that can cause problems for themselves and others. The most common challenges are due to a lack of assertiveness in situations that call for speaking up and being heard. Doves sometimes feel intimidated in situations that may involve friction or the threat of conflict. By withdrawing or remaining silent, they may fail to get what they want, and their opinions may not be heard. When this happens, doves may become resentful and see themselves as martyrs or become dependent on others to protect their interests.

Doves' strong people orientation can get in the way of completing tasks in a timely manner and with optimal results. The wish to avoid conflict can lead to accepting mediocre work and avoiding decision making. This is a great disadvantage when they are in positions in which they are expected to set standards and take a leadership role. Doves sometimes also have difficulty in exercising authority in situations in which they are accountable for others' results and may end up being too lenient when discipline and firmness are required.

The Strong Dove's Strengths

The following qualities and characteristics are strengths of the dove style that can be emphasized and leveraged to advantage in a variety of situations and relationships.

- **Contemplative** – Being thoughtful, calm, and relaxed; thinking things through rather than rushing to conclusions.
- **Group-Oriented** – Working well on group tasks and in teams; helping facilitate teamwork while accomplishing goals and making decisions; willing to recognize and give credit to group efforts rather than seeking individual recognition.
- **Cooperative** – Willing to seek consensus and "win-win" solutions rather than competing to serve their own interests or trying to persuade others to give up theirs; willing to share resources to achieve a common goal.
- **Stable** – Maintaining an "even keel" of emotions and manner; avoiding extremes in moods; being reliably steady in responses to most situations, even those that may be stressful or unpleasant.
- **Patient** – Remaining calm and accepting of others' flaws or failings; allowing time for others to complete their thoughts and present ideas in their own way; maintaining an even emotional state in situations others might find frustrating or exasperating.
- **Unselfish** – Supportive of others' needs; putting others' concerns and interests before their own; freely sharing resources, credit, and recognition with others rather than seeking their own advancement.
- **Nurturing** – Offering support and help to others, especially those who are new, inexperienced, or struggling to learn and grow.
- **Consistent** – Being reliable in how they react and respond to other people; following through on promises and commitments.

The Strong Dove's Interpersonal Challenges

As is often the case, great strengths can also be manifested as potential weaknesses. The following are some common characteristics observed in extreme doves when they are at their least effective:

- **Easily Intimidated** – Responding to friction, conflict, or aggression with meekness or compliance, sometimes to their own disadvantage; failing to speak up for their own interests or the interests of others; lack of confidence in the face of others' assertiveness, leading to loss of self-esteem.
- **Procrastination** – Putting off tasks that need to be done; finding excuses to avoid taking action; delaying responses to situations that require more immediate and decisive action.
- **Dependency** – Over reliance on others' approval or permission rather than acting on their own to get something done; relying on someone else's authority rather than taking responsibility or accountability for decisions or actions; consistently letting others take the lead rather than stepping forward to take initiative when something needs doing.
- **Being a Martyr** – Allowing others to take advantage of them rather than asserting their own interests; feeling put upon or abused by others even though they have not clearly asked for help; resenting others for unfair treatment despite the fact that they may be unaware of what the dove wanted.
- **Being Too Lenient** – Failing to exert authority in situations in which it is their responsibility to set standards or provide discipline; avoiding action to correct disruptive behaviors of others that might undermine the quality or results of the group; avoiding giving feedback or input that would help bring about improvements due to shyness or fear of conflict.
- **Avoiding Engagement** – Pulling back physically from uncomfortable social situations or situations in which there is conflict or a threat of friction with others; remaining silent and unresponsive in certain situations.
- **Stubbornness** – Appearing resistant because of fear of offending others or the possibility of friction or controversy; appearing to block an action or change, primarily in order to avoid anticipated criticism or disagreement.
- **Being Too Sensitive** – Overreacting to perceived slights; attaching negative meanings to situations or statements when there are no grounds for the negative interpretation; having feelings easily hurt by small mistakes or innocent remarks.

Increasing Interpersonal Effectiveness for Strong Doves

Here are some suggestions to leverage your strengths and avoid potential interpersonal pitfalls in common work situations such as meetings, team interactions, supervising others, and giving feedback.

Cultivate decision-making skills

- Whether you are in a team or leadership position, consciously review and identify your own information, experience, and opinions, and be ready to state them clearly and unambiguously as part of a decision discussion.

- When it is your responsibility to make a decision, set a deadline for announcing your choice, and prepare a clear statement of the decision and the rationale for it. Tell others when to expect your announcement and stick to it.

- If you are unsure about how to make good decisions in complex situations, develop your knowledge and skills by reading articles or boo or attending a workshop or seminar. Learn a process for identifying and choosing among options.

Develop independent thinking and acting

- Analyze situations in your work and life where you have waited for someone else to take the lead and see what those situations have in common. Ask yourself:
  - Did you lack information or experience that would have helped you take independent action?
  - Were you uncertain of whether you had the authority or right to take action on your own?
  - Did you feel it was too risky to take independent action for which there could possibly be negative consequences?
  - Did you simply lack confidence in your own ability to make a good decision about which action to take?

- Once you have identified potential issues that keep you from acting independently, set a goal for taking independent action in at least

two or three situations in which you might otherwise feel dependent on others. Make sure you:
- Gather information you need to make a decision or take action.
- Clarify that you have the authority to act independently if you need to.
- Reduce the risks of negative consequences by planning ahead for responding to contingencies.

▷ Practice making independent decisions and taking actions in non-threatening situations at first, and share your results with a friend, manager, or mentor who can help you recognize the benefits and good results of your independence.

⊘ Overcome tendency to be too sensitive

▷ Manage your self-talk to give yourself positive messages about others' intentions and the meaning of their remarks or actions.

▷ If you find yourself reacting to a remark or behavior defensively or with hurt feelings, stop and analyze the situation and context. Consider possible alternative explanations for the remark.

▷ If you feel you have been slighted or treated unfairly, think through the specifics of what has happened and then plan a conversation with the person or people involved.
- In an unemotional, calm manner, describe your feelings without attributing motives or attitudes to the other person.
- Ask the person to respond with his or her interpretation of the situation. Listen attentively without interrupting.
- If it appears that there is indeed a problem, ask for help in avoiding the problem in the future or correcting the situation.
- Agree on a possible solution.

⊘ Develop habits to overcome procrastination

▷ Keep a journal or diary to identify situations in which you are procrastinating, whether delaying a decision or putting off an action that needs to be taken. Analyze each situation to identify the primary reasons for your reluctance to act. Answer the following:
- Are you concerned about possible negative reactions from people who will be affected?
- Are you unsure of what action or decision to take because you don't have good information or haven't thought it through?
- Are you simply putting off the action because it seems burdensome or time consuming?

➡ Identify three priority actions that need to be taken in the next 30 days, and set a specific deadline, making sure it is reasonable and achievable.

➡ For each deadline, identify what needs to happen for you to take action: Gather more information? Think through how you can minimize negative reactions? Make a more explicit plan to delegate some aspect of the action to be taken?

➡ When you have met your first deadline, review what went well and what you want to do differently to ensure you are on schedule for the next decision or action. Adjust your approach.

Understanding the Extreme Turtle

Your responses indicate that your style is that of an "extreme" turtle, suggesting that you display the characteristics of the turtle style very intensely.

You are very much an introvert, drawing energy from your internal thoughts and reflections. You are more task-oriented than people-oriented and often need time alone to think and reflect. You usually prefer to work in private rather than in shared space or in the company of groups of people.

Because you are naturally inclined toward gathering data and thinking things through in a systematic and logical fashion, you are highly effective at analyzing complex problems and identifying the best solutions. With your attention to detail and insistence on accuracy, it is very probable that your work consistently meets high standards of quality and completeness.   Your ability to analyze information and organize it in the form of charts and graphs give you an advantage in presenting data to others in an understandable format.

The people who interact with you at work and in social situations will notice that you use precise language and speak in a quiet, controlled tone of voice. You are known for thinking things through with care. When confronted with an issue or problem to be solved, you like to explore all aspects and consider multiple options before arriving at a final decision or solution.

Extreme turtles sometimes face challenges that come with the core tendencies of their style. When stressed, the extreme turtle's concern for detail and the natural desire to gather facts and data can produce "analysis paralysis," with research and data gathering taking the place of making a decision. When this happens, extreme turtles can be perceived as slow, bogged down in detail, and generally ineffective. Because extreme turtles value organization and a systematic approach to getting things done, they can become "set in their ways." They become resistant to change and narrow-minded when it comes to innovation or new ideas. When others fail to meet their high standards of accuracy and perfectionism, they appear critical and picky, overly obsessed with details others find less important.

The Extreme Turtle's Strengths

The following qualities and characteristics are strengths of the turtle style you have in abundance that can be emphasized and leveraged to advantage in a variety of situations and relationships.

- **Analytical** – Taking a deliberate, thoughtful approach to problems and issues; breaking complex situations into parts to determine what the issues are and decide how to address each issue; looking for the causes and contributing factors to problems before attempting to develop a solution.
- **Reflective** – Forming ideas, opinions, and solutions based on thinking things through independently; internally considering subject matter, ideas, or purpose that lead to well-thought-out conclusions.
- **Well Organized** – Neat and orderly in terms of both thinking and physical surroundings; placing things in a predictable sequence; sorting ideas and things into logical categories that have a clear rationale for being grouped together; linking ideas into a hierarchical structure that is easy for others to understand and follow.
- **Logical** – Using reasoning and evidence more than intuition to think things through; being organized in thinking; avoiding jumping to conclusions without a factual basis.
- **Accurate** – Being careful to ensure information is correct; concern with verifying data and other kinds of information to confirm that it reflects reality; avoiding exaggeration or overstatement in favor of precise language.
- **Conscientious** – Being responsible and careful; thinking ahead to anticipate consequences of actions; concerned to follow protocols and procedures; doing "the right thing right."
- **Systematic** – Using a methodical, step-by-step approach to decisions and actions; following a procedure to achieve a goal; using a proven approach to achieve similar goals rather than making up a new method or process each time.
- **Detail-Oriented** – Concerned with specifics rather than just the "big picture" when dealing with plans, projects, actions to be taken; being exacting about following steps and using the correct tools rather than accepting approximations or estimates.

The Extreme Turtle's Interpersonal Challenges

As is often the case, great strengths can also be manifested as potential weaknesses. The following are some common characteristics observed in extreme turtles when they are at their least effective:

- **Isolating** – Excluding others; operating too independently; avoiding interactions with others; being perceived as aloof or cold; being perceived as disliking the company of others; acting alone when others might expect to be included or to have a role.

- **Avoids Decisions** – Focusing on fact gathering and analysis instead of moving forward to a goal; delaying a decision beyond the point where additional information affects the outcome of the decision; delaying announcing a final decision; waiting to make a decision until there is no longer a need for the decision or until someone else makes it.

- **Critical** – Finding fault with others' ideas; making unfavorable or belittling observations or remarks; making suggestions for improvement that imply rejection of what has been done.

- **Narrow-Minded** – Being closed to new ideas or innovative approaches; responding favorably to only a very limited range of choices or options; being predisposed to rejecting an idea rather than looking for reasons to accept or try it out.

- **Obsessive** – Overly persistent in pursuing an idea or method to the exclusion of other considerations or concerns; unable to "let go" of an idea or position even after being shown reasons for moving on or forgetting about it; returning repeatedly to the same argument, detail, or point of view, even after others have decided not to pursue it.

- **Avoids Change** – Resisting anything new or different; tendency to reject change; unwilling to adapt to different methods, technology, job requirements, or new environments, sometimes to their own or others' disadvantage.

- **Picky** – Overly critical; focusing on very small details or concerns that don't make a difference in outcome or quality; insisting on perfection when perfection is difficult to achieve and not required by the circumstances; insisting that others spend time making multiple corrections or revisions even when there are unlikely to be productive results from the time being spent doing so.

- **Poor Adaptability** – Difficulty in adapting to others' preferred styles, especially those that are more people-oriented and assertive; being resistant and critical rather than opening minded towards others with different styles.

Increasing Interpersonal Effectiveness for Extreme Turtles

Here are some suggestions to leverage your strengths and avoid potential interpersonal pitfalls in common work situations such as meetings, team interactions, supervising others, and giving feedback.

◎ Develop balanced feedback skills

➡️ When you are required to give an opinion or are asked for input, look first for what is right or has gone well, and balance any negative or unfavorable comments with positive, favorable remarks.

➡️ Go out of your way to compliment others when the opportunity arises, being specific and timely in commenting on something good that has been said or done by a friend, family member, or member of your work group.

➡️ Keep your comments objective and based on what is observable and/or behavioral rather than focusing on what you believe to be a person's motives or attitudes.

➡️ If you are in a position to give feedback to help someone make corrections or changes, make this an occasion for a two-way conversation:

- Ask the person what he or she thinks went well and could be done differently.
- Add your comments to what the other person says.
- Ask for suggestions about changes that could bring about improvements.
- Add your own suggestions and agree on what changes to make.

◎ Increase level of people-oriented behaviors and activities

➡️ If you are in an environment in which people typically socialize during lunch hours or breaks, make an effort to join in these conversations at least once or twice a week, even if this is not your normal inclination.

➡️ Look for opportunities to become a member of a task force or team that has a group assignment, and make it a point to volunteer for a team assignment in which you will be working with at least one or two other people to achieve the goal.

➡ Ask for feedback from a colleague or co-worker on a project or plan you are working on, and incorporate at least one suggestion into your work.

➡ Look for an opportunity to share some area of your knowledge or expertise with others, or volunteer to help a new or inexperienced person learn about something you do well such as using a software application, preparing a particular report, etc.

◎ Work to make decisions and take action in a timely manner

➡ Keep in mind that there is no way to perfectly predict all possible consequences and outcomes or reduce all risk to zero.

➡ When you have a decision to make or an action to take, set a specific deadline for when you will make the final decision. Plan your preliminary analysis and research to be completed in time for the deadline.

➡ If you begin to feel you don't have enough data or analysis finished to make a decision, ask others to assess what you have. If others feel there is sufficient information, take action based on what you have.

➡ Follow a systematic process for decision making, allotting a specific amount of time for completing each step:

- Set criteria for what a good decision will look like (what outcomes you want from the decision or what features a good solution will need to have).
- Focus analysis and information gathering around how well each option fits the criteria rather than simply accumulating undifferentiated background information.
- Ask for input from people who have expertise and knowledge about the subject at hand.
- Use a numerical weighting system to help you match options against the criteria you have set, and use the scores to help you move forward with a choice.

➡ Identify some less consequential decisions and actions whereby you can practice making a choice by intuition alone, testing the outcomes compared to cases in which you spent a lot of time thinking and gathering information ahead of time.

◉ Practice adaptability

▸ When you have opportunities to consider new approaches, ideas, or methodologies, think first of possible benefits, advantages, and reasons to adopt the new idea rather than reasons to reject it.

▸ When interacting with others, make an effort to observe and respond to indicators of feelings, and try to identify how the other person is reacting -- especially in situations in which people may feel upset, frustrated, or angry. Be direct in addressing these issues.

▸ Ask a checking question to let the person know you are paying attention to how he or she feels, such as, "Are you still comfortable with this?" "Are you o.k. with how we are proceeding?" "Is there something different we can be doing that is more comfortable for you?"

▸ Use a testing statement to see if it helps the other person to share feelings, such as, "Many people find this kind of situation frustrating. Do you have that kind of reaction?"

◉ Work on being more open and straightforward about discussing your own feelings.

▸ Share how you are feeling in appropriate situations, expressing your satisfaction or pleasure when something goes well, and being willing to acknowledge your own frustration or dissatisfaction when things aren't going well.

▸ Make empathic statements to acknowledge others' feelings, such as, "I understand why you would feel upset in this situation," or "From what you just said, it sounds as if you are feeling angry about this decision. If it happened to me, I think I would feel the same way."

◉ When dealing with peacocks in particular, you will have more successful interactions if you are open to their ideas and do the following:

▸ Listen patiently while they express ideas and feelings, and look for positive comments you can add to the conversation.

▸ Maintain an open mind when you hear ideas and concepts that may not initially appear to have enough facts or data to back them up. Remember: there can be merit in new, innovative approaches.

- Go out of your way to express appreciation for creative approaches that have good outcomes.
- Engage in a real two-way conversation to offer constructive suggestions, ideas, and ways to improve an idea or proposal. Use an open, assertive style that shows you are listening and sincerely care about the success of the idea or project.
- Ask for their input and thoughts about choices, actions, and decisions you might be making, and provide recognition for their contributions.

Understanding the Strong Turtle

Your responses indicate that your style is that of a turtle, suggesting that you tend to be introverted and draw energy from your internal thoughts and reflections. You are more task-oriented than people-oriented, and sometimes need to be alone to think and reflect. When it is up to you, you likely prefer to work more of the time in private rather than in shared space or in the company of groups of people.

Because you are naturally inclined toward gathering data and thinking things through in a systematic and logical fashion, you are effective at analyzing complex problems and identifying the best solutions. With your attention to detail and concern for accuracy, your work is likely characterized by quality and completeness. Your ability to analyze information and organize it in the form of charts and graphs can give you an advantage in presenting data to others in an understandable format.

The people who interact with you in work and social situations will probably notice that you use more precise language and speak in a quiet, controlled tone of voice. People know that you like to think things through carefully and consider multiple options before arriving at a final decision or solution.

Turtles can face challenges when interacting with others. When stressed, turtles may overdo their concern for details, and their desire to gather facts and data can produce "analysis paralysis." When this happens, research and data gathering take the place of making a decision, with the result that they are seen as slow and bogged down in detail. Turtles can also be perceived as "set in their ways" when they place too much value on using a familiar, systematic approach, and become resistant to change and narrow-minded about innovation and new ideas. When others fail to meet their high standards of accuracy and perfectionism, their concerns can appear critical and picky; they seem overly obsessed with details that others find less important.

The Strong Turtle's Strengths

The following qualities and characteristics are strengths of the turtle style that can be emphasized and leveraged to advantage in a variety of situations and relationships.

- **Analytical** – Taking a deliberate, thoughtful approach to problems and issues; breaking down complex situations to determine what the issues are and decide how to address each issue; looking for the causes and contributing factors before attempting to develop a solution.
- **Reflective** – Forming ideas, opinions, and solutions based on thinking things through independently; internally considering subject matter, idea, or purpose that leads to well-thought-out conclusions.
- **Well Organized** – Neat and orderly in terms of both thinking and physical surroundings; placing things in a predictable sequence; sorting ideas and things into logical categories that have a clear rationale for being grouped together; linking ideas into a hierarchical structure that is easy for others to understand and follow.
- **Logical** – Using reasoning and evidence more than intuition to think things through; being organized in thinking; avoiding jumping to conclusions without a factual basis.
- **Accurate** – Ensuring information is correct; concerned with verifying data and other kinds of information; avoiding exaggeration or overstatement in favor of precise language.
- **Conscientious** – Being responsible and careful; thinking ahead to anticipate consequences of actions; doing "the right thing right."
- **Systematic** – Using a methodical, step-by-step approach to decisions and actions; following a procedure to achieve a goal.
- **Detail-Oriented** – Concerned with specifics rather than just the "big picture" when dealing with plans and projects; being exacting rather than accepting approximations or estimates.

The Strong Turtle's Interpersonal Challenges

As is often the case, great strengths can also be manifested as potential weaknesses. The following are some common characteristics observed in turtles when they are at their least effective:

- **Isolating** – Excluding others; operating too independently; avoiding interactions with others; being perceived as aloof or cold; being perceived as disliking the company of others; acting alone when others might expect to be included or to have a role.

- **Avoids Decisions** – Focusing on fact gathering and analysis instead of moving toward a goal; delaying a decision beyond the point at which additional information affects the outcome of the decision; delaying announcement of a final decision; waiting to make a decision until there is no longer a need for the decision or until someone else makes it.

- **Critical** – Finding fault with others' ideas; making unfavorable or belittling observations or remarks; making suggestions for improvement that imply rejection of what has been done.

- **Narrow-Minded** – Being closed to new ideas or innovative approaches; responding favorably to only a very limited range of choices or options; being predisposed to reject an idea rather than looking for reasons to accept or try it out.

- **Obsessive** – Overly persistent in pursuing an idea or method to the exclusion of other considerations or concerns; unable to "let go" of an idea or position even after being shown reasons for moving on or forgetting about it; returning repeatedly to the same argument, detail, or point of view, even after others have decided not to pursue it.

  Avoids Change – Resistance to anything new or different; tendency to reject change; unwilling to adapt to different methods, technology, job requirements, or new environments, sometimes to their own and others' disadvantage.

- **Picky** – Overly critical; focusing on very small details or concerns that don't make a difference in outcome or quality; insisting on perfection when perfection is difficult to achieve and not required by the circumstances; insisting that others spend time making multiple corrections or revisions even when it is unlikely the results from such effort would be productive.

- **Unforgiving** – Unyielding, inflexible; unwilling to make allowances for weaknesses or errors; refusal to recognize good intentions when the outcome is not what is wanted; holding others to unrealistically high standards.

Increasing Interpersonal Effectiveness for Strong Turtles

Here are some suggestions to leverage your strengths and avoid potential interpersonal pitfalls in common work situations such as meetings, team interactions, supervising others, and giving feedback.

Develop balanced feedback skills

- When you are required to give an opinion or are asked for input, look first for what is right or has gone well, and balance any negative or unfavorable comments with positive, favorable remarks.
- Go out of your way to compliment others when the opportunity arises, being specific and timely in commenting on something good that has been said or done by a friend, family member, or member of your work group.
- Keep your comments objective and based on what is observable and/or behavioral rather than focusing on what you believe to be a person's motives or attitudes.
- If you are in a position to give feedback to help someone make corrections or changes, make this an occasion for a two-way conversation:
  - Ask the person what he or she thinks went well or could be done differently.
  - Add your comments to what the other person says.
  - Ask for suggestions about changes that could bring about improvements.
  - Add your own suggestions and agree on what changes to make.

Increase level of people-oriented behaviors and activities

- If you are in an environment in which people typically socialize during lunch hours or breaks, make an effort to join in these conversations at least once or twice a week, even if this is not your normal inclination.
- Look for opportunities to become a member of a task force or team that has a group assignment and make it a point to volunteer for a

team assignment whereby you will be working with at least one or two other people to achieve the goal.

- Ask for feedback from a colleague or co-worker on a project or plan you are working on and incorporate at least one suggestion into your work.
- Look for an opportunity to share some area of your knowledge or expertise with others, or volunteer to help a new or inexperienced person learn about something you do well such as using a software application, preparing a particular report, etc.

Work to make decisions and take action in a timely manner

- Keep in mind that there is no way to perfectly predict all possible consequences and outcomes or reduce all risk to zero.
- When you have a decision to make or an action to take, set a specific deadline for when you will make the final decision. Plan your preliminary analysis and research to be completed in time for the deadline.
- If you begin to feel you don't have enough data or analysis finished to make a decision, ask others to assess what you have. If they feel there is sufficient information, take action based on what you have.
- Follow a systematic process for decision making, allotting a specific amount of time for completing each step:
  - Set criteria for what a good decision will look like (what outcomes you want from the decision or what features a good solution will need to have).
  - Focus analysis and information gathering around how well each option fits the criteria rather than simply accumulating undifferentiated background information.
  - Ask for input from people who have expertise and knowledge about the subject at hand.
  - Use a numerical weighting system to help you match options against the criteria you have set, and use the scores to help you move forward with a choice.
- Identify some less consequential decisions and actions by which you can practice making a choice by intuition alone, testing the outcomes compared to cases in which you spent a lot of time thinking and gathering information ahead of time.

◉ Practice being open-minded and willing to embrace change

➡ When you have opportunities to consider new approaches, ideas, or methodologies, think first of possible benefits, advantages, and reasons to adopt the new idea rather than reasons to reject it.

➡ If you initially feel yourself resisting a proposed change, take some time to sort through your reasons and objections, and look for positive steps you can take or suggest to address those issues. Look for a chance to be the initiator of ideas for change that you can support, such as improvements in processes or procedures, or a new method for achieving an existing goal or objective. Volunteer to be part of a team or task force assigned to implement a change, and use your analytical and organizing skills to help develop a plan that will ensure the change is successful.

Opposite Styles

Your profile, representing two opposite styles, is rare enough to suggest that there could be value in getting some additional input from others as a check and balance to the results from your questionnaire. This could be done through using a "360" degree feedback or other assessment instrument to get feedback from a group of co-workers or peers with whom you interact regularly in a consistent role.

Result for People with All Four Styles

Your responses indicate that you demonstrate characteristics of all four of the styles: lion, peacock, dove, and turtle. Since some of the characteristics of these styles are contradictory, this is a quite unusual profile. It may mean that you are extremely adaptable and able to adjust your style to accommodate to other styles with great ease and versatility.

As a summary, each of the four styles has characteristics that you may be demonstrating in your interactions with different groups of people.

⊘ Understanding Lions

When you are in lion mode, for example, you show the characteristics of an extrovert. You like to participate in activities that include other people, though in your work mode you tend to be more task-oriented than people-oriented. Lion qualities of courage, decisiveness, and confidence may make you a natural leader, and the ability to think strategically and independently gives an advantage in achieving the results that are important to lions.

The main challenge for lions is to avoid appearing dictatorial and intimidating, which can cause others to perceive the lion style as being bossy rather than leading in a positive way

⊘ Understanding Peacocks

A peacock is also an extrovert but with a notably different set of style characteristics. Peacocks are usually lively and friendly in work and social situations and bring humor, enthusiasm, and energy into your relationships. Since peacocks tend to be creative and visionary, your peacock characteristics likely make it easy for you to generate new ideas. The peacock's skill at influencing others can help you gain support and cooperation for getting things done.

When stressed, peacocks can sometimes express their feelings intensely in a way that creates tension and may harm relationships. Peacocks can also find it difficult to finish as many projects as they start, and sometime they overlook details others see as important. When this happens, peacocks can be perceived as careless, irresponsible, or superficial.

⚙ Understanding Doves

Unlike the lion and the peacock, doves are more introverts than extrovert, meaning that they often attend to their inner world of ideas and impressions, and may sometimes need time alone to think things through and "recharge" their energy. In their work mode, however, they are people oriented more than task oriented and like to support and nurture others.

Your dove characteristics can make you an effective team player, taking a cooperative and supportive approach to getting things done. In stressful conditions, you may be effective at maintaining self-control and stability rather than giving in to your emotions. Doves are often able to exercise natural diplomatic skills to help avoid conflict and friction, which often make them uncomfortable. In social situations, they are usually easygoing, relaxed, and likeable, making others feel comfortable and at ease.

When doves are not at their best, they face challenges that can cause problems for themselves and others. Unlike lions, the most common challenges are due to a lack of assertiveness in situations that call for speaking up and being heard. Doves sometimes feel intimidated in situations that may involve friction or the threat of conflict. By withdrawing or remaining silent, they may fail to get what they want, and their opinions may not be heard.

⚙ Understanding Turtles

Like the dove, turtles tend to be introverted, drawing energy from internal thoughts and reflections. Turtles are more task oriented than people oriented and sometimes need to be alone to think and reflect--the opposite of a Peacock. Turtles often prefer to work more of the time in private rather than in shared space or in the company of groups of people.

 Turtles are naturally inclined toward gathering data and thinking things through in a systematic and logical fashion, making them effective at analyzing complex problems and identifying the best solutions. The turtle's attention to detail and concern for accuracy ensures that their work is usually characterized by quality and completeness.

When stressed, turtles may overdo their concern for details, and their desire to gather facts and data can produce "analysis paralysis." When this happens, research and data-gathering take the place of making a decision, with the result that they are seen as slow and bogged down in detail. Turtles can also be perceived as "set in their ways" when they place too much value on using a familiar, systematic approach and become resistant to change and narrow-minded about innovation and new ideas.

The Lion's Strengths

The following qualities and characteristics are strengths of the lion style that can be leveraged to advantage in a variety of situations and relationships.

Assertiveness – Willing to speak up, express wishes clearly, and state desires without being intimidated by others.

Results Oriented – Focusing on clear goals and standards for achievement; seeking the most direct path to tangible payoffs for any endeavor; impatient with fuzzy or unclear objectives; not liking to waste time on efforts that seem less likely to produce concrete results.

The Lion's Interpersonal Challenges

As is often the case, our strengths can be connected to potential weaknesses. The following are some common characteristics observed in lions when they are not at their best.

Aggressive – Quick to push back or go on the attack; seen as domineering.

Impatient – Finding it challenging to focus and concentrate for long periods of time.

The Peacock's Strengths

The following qualities and characteristics are strengths of the peacock style that can be emphasized and leveraged for positive results in a variety of situations and relationships.

Gregarious – Sociable, outgoing; finding it easy to strike up conversations and develop relationships and networks; conversing confidently with a variety of people, including strangers in new settings; can be the "life of the party," the center of attention, and a leader of social activities.

Energetic – Being action oriented and forceful in tackling tasks; taking the initiative to bring about an effect or reach a goal.

The Peacock's Interpersonal Challenges

The following are some common characteristics observed in peacocks when they are at their least effective.

Verbose – Dominating the conversation, taking too long to get to the point, not considering others' interests and preferences.

Irresponsible – Evading accountability for tasks or not accepting the consequences of their actions; failing to anticipate and plan for contingencies or problems; letting others down by lack of foresight; failing to share in creating solutions for problems.

The Dove's Strengths

The following qualities and characteristics are strengths of the dove style that can be emphasized and leveraged to advantage in a variety of situations and relationships.

Contemplative – Being thoughtful, calm, and relaxed; thinking things through rather than rushing to conclusions.

Group-Oriented – Working well on group tasks and in teams; helping facilitate team decision making; willing to recognize and give credit to group efforts rather than seeking individual recognition.

The Dove's Interpersonal Challenges

The following are some common characteristics observed in extreme doves when they are at their least effective.

Easily Intimidated – Responding to friction, conflict, or aggression with meekness or compliance, sometimes to their own disadvantage; failing to speak up for their own interests or the interests of others; lack of confidence in the face of others' assertiveness, leading to loss of self-esteem.

Procrastination – Putting off tasks that need to be done; finding excuses to avoid taking action; delaying responses to situations that require more immediate and decisive action.

The Strong Turtle's Strengths

The following qualities and characteristics are strengths of the turtle style that can be emphasized and leveraged to advantage in a variety of situations and relationships.

Analytical – Taking a deliberate, thoughtful approach to problems and issues; breaking down complex situations to determine what the issues are and decide how to address each issue; looking for the causes and contributing factors before attempting to develop a solution.

Reflective – Forming ideas, opinions, and solutions based on thinking things through independently; internally considering-subject matter, idea, or purpose that leads to well-thought-out conclusions.

◎ The Turtle's Interpersonal Challenges

The following are some common characteristics observed in turtles when they are at their least effective:

Isolating – Excluding others; operating too independently; avoiding interactions with others; being perceived as aloof or cold; being perceived as disliking the company of others; acting alone when others might expect to be included or to have a role.

Avoids Decisions – Focusing on fact gathering and analysis instead of moving towards a goal; delaying a decision beyond the point at which additional information affects the outcome of the decision; delaying announcement of a final decision; waiting to make a decision until there is no longer a need for the decision or until someone else makes it.

Increasing the Accuracy of Your Profile

Your rare profile suggests that there could be value in getting some additional input from others. This could be done through using a "360" degree feedback or assessment instrument to get feedback from a group of co-workers or peers with whom you interact regularly in a consistent role.

Your Score Explained

Jungle Escape

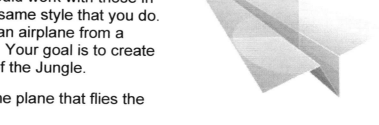

For this activity, you should work with those in the room who have the same style that you do. Your team must create an airplane from a piece of flipchart paper. Your goal is to create a plane that will fly out of the Jungle.

The team that creates the plane that flies the farthest wins.

You will have five minutes to discuss how you will build the plane. You will then be given the paper. You will have five minutes to build the plane. You will launch your plane when asked to do so by the facilitator.

Jungle Escape Debrief

Debrief Questions

1. Did you enjoy working with a group of people all of the same style?

   ◎ What were the benefits?

   ◎ What were the drawbacks?

2. Did you find yourself taking on traits from other styles to accommodate those who shared your dominant style?

Alligator River

In teams of five or six, you must cross Alligator River, home to some of the largest and hungriest alligators in the world.

The River is the longest part of the room. Your group must get each of the members from one side of the room to the other without touching the bare floor or carpet.

Each team has two rafts (flipchart paper). Team members may cross the river as often as needed.

The team that gets all members from one side of the room to the other the fastest without touching the river wins.

Alligator River Debrief

Debrief Questions

1. How did you determine how you would get the members of your team across Alligator River? What factors did you consider?

2. Do you regularly consider the strengths of others when working together on projects?

Jungle Boogie

Working in groups, choose a popular song as the theme song for each of the Jungle animals.

LION

PEACOCK

DOVE

TURTLE

Habitat

Your team has recently inherited a house that once belonged to a very famous national hero. Unfortunately, the house has fallen into disrepair. Your goal is to sell the property.

The house sits on 180 acres in the country. It needs about $650,000 worth of work to restore it back to its former glory. You have four prospective buyers. Interestingly, they are all related to the original owner. Each of them prefers a different style.

Your task is to determine what benefits you would highlight to each of the prospective buyers. You many add information to the facts listed above to help make your case.

LION

PEACOCK

DOVE

TURTLE

Jungle Invention

You and your team work in product development for Jungle Industries, a company that invents style improvement products. Your team is tasked today with creating a product to improve communication for one of the Jungle animals. The product can either enhance a positive trait or compensate for one of the challenges faced by members with that style.

You will use flipchart paper and markers to outline your product. You have 20 minutes to complete the activity.

You will then present your results to the whole group.

Case Studies

Case One:

You are working with a dove and you are a lion. What might be some possible sources of conflict? How should you adapt your style?

Case Two:

You are a turtle/dove working with a mixed group. What might you have to do to adapt your style?

Case Three:

You are a peacock working with a bunch of non-peacocks. What behaviors should you tone down? What value do you bring to the group?

Case Four:

Tony the turtle is very slow and methodical in his work. This is very annoying to Larry lion and Petunia peacock. What can Larry and Petunia do to improve their situation? Is there any action they can take to hurry Tony along?

Case Five:

Donna dove never complains about much. However, you sense that something is wrong with your relationship with her. What can you do to find out what she thinks? What type of body language and pacing should you adopt?

Case Six:

What behaviors can you exhibit to improve relationships with lions? Peacocks? Doves? Turtles?

Case Seven:

When working with a mixed group, what style should you address first? Why?

Case Eight:

Is there a style to which you find it particularly challenging to adapt? Why? What will you do to overcome this challenge?

Don't Get Eaten Alive

You and your team are preparing for a group meeting with all of the styles in the Jungle. The meeting is about and acquisition of another organization that is smaller than your own. Over the next year, the group should expect a lot of changes.

Already, the rumors are flying. Your job is to figure out how to present the information to each group of people. You should also consider any possible problems you might encounter. Furthermore, you should suggest any tips you can think of to improve the facilitation of the meeting.

LIONS

PEACOCKS

DOVES

TURTLES

Problems to Watch For:

Facilitation Suggestions:

Jungle Team

Team Member	Preferred Style	Strengths	Needs

Jungle Team

Plot your team's style on the chart below.

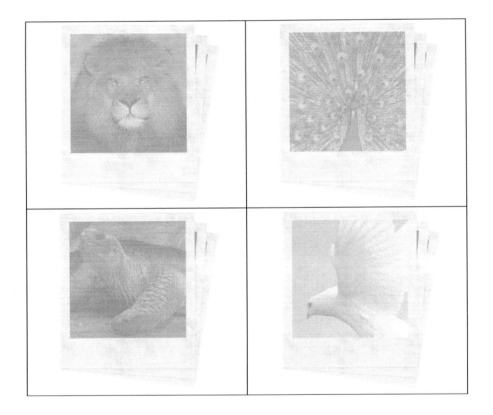

- What do we need to start doing?

- What do we need to stop doing?

- What do we need to continue doing?

Feedback Safari

Coaching and developing employees is part science and part art, and depending on your style and the style of the other person, the equation is never quite the same.

What's the Science?

The science of feedback involves consistently following a process.

- First, those who report to you should understand that feedback will benefit both them and the organization.
- Second, they should receive it both formally and informally on a regular basis.
- Third, they must feel as if you follow up and take interest in their development.

1. How have you communicated to those who report to you that you will give feedback regularly? Specifically, what did you say?

2. How often do you give formal and informal feedback? When was the last time you did each?

3. What actions demonstrate to employees that you have an interest in their development?

Stories of Survival

Review the two stories below. Which one is most like you?

Roger Costanzia is a vice president at his company. He is 45 years old and comfortable in his career. The company has always run "lean and mean." Consequently, Roger is often pulled in many directions. He supervises four people. Two of them work in an office about ten miles away. However, he does not see them but every two weeks or so. Over the years Roger has had some success with those who report to him, but some of the others have not performed as he had expected. Roger has been promoted many times within his own career. With his current workload, he is not able to give those who report to him the attention they deserve. Today, in fact, Maria Green had a meeting scheduled to talk to him about a project she is working on. Roger canceled it because of something due for a client. After all, he figures, Marie is smart and will figure it out.

Lori O'Malley is a director at a large hospital. She has worked there for the last seven years. She is busy and often finds herself working late. She has five direct reports. She meets with each of them every two weeks for 30 minutes each without fail. During those meetings she follows a specific agenda and reviews items she has saved for discussion throughout the week. Her staff has turned over several times. However, this has happened not because they have quit but because many of them have been promoted to other areas within the hospital. Today she is meeting with Greg Bowman for the first time. Greg was transferred to Lori's department from another area. He doesn't really know what to expect. Lori explains that they will meet each week to discuss projects. She asks him to think about his position in the hospital and what he would like to do over the next year, over the next two years, and over the next five years. At their next meeting, Greg is to bring that information back to her.

Many of us are part Roger and part Lori. If the situation is difficult, we follow Roger's model. When it is less challenging, on the other hand, we find it easier to be more like Lori. In addition to adhering to the science of scheduling, routine, and preparation, this is where understanding the art of feedback can help us.

What's the Art?

The art of counseling and coaching is getting comfortable with delivering feedback and positioning what you say in a way that it will be well received by the person you are speaking with.

Okay, that's easy to say, but how do you do that?

- First, recognize where you are and what challenges you have.
- Second, determine who you are dealing with, and PLAN. PLAN. PLAN.
- Third, take the plunge.

Survival Challenge

You have an employee who is not performing well. However, you have not spent much time mentoring him. You've avoided saying anything in the past, but now you feel like you have to.

- What are some of the reasons for not saying something in the past?

- What is the worst thing that could happen if you do say something?

Feedback Safari Map

Using what you have just read and what we have discussed to guide your thinking, complete the chart below.

Me	Person X
My Style	**His/Her Style**
Biggest Challenge for Me	**Predicted Reaction**
My Opening Statement (Think about how you will tailor your message.)	
Questions I Will Ask Person X	
When I Will Do This	
How I Will Follow Up	

Personal Action Plan

My Style Strengths Are:

The Primary Value I Bring to a Team Is:

My Opportunities for Improvement Are:

The Three Actions I Plan to Take Based on What I've Learned:

Quick Reference

	LIONS	**PEACOCKS**	**DOVES**	**TURTLES**
KEYWORD	Dominance, Results, Driven	Image, Fun, Enthusiasm	Steady, Supportive, Cooperative	Correct, Careful, Conscientious
QUESTIONS	WHAT Questions	WHO Questions	HOW Questions	WHY Questions
DO	- Get to the point. - Be specific. - Be logical. - Provide choices, options, and recommendations. - Stick to business. - Tell more, ask less. - Speak up for yourself. - When writing, keep it short. - Be on time. - Expect them to "tell it like it is."	- Allow time to socialize. - Be fun and fast paced. - Ask for their opinions. - Talk about ideas. - Make decisions quickly. - When writing, keep it short and sweet. - Respond quickly. - Demonstrate high energy.	- Move casually and informally. - Be patient. - Show that you have considered others' feelings. - Give them time to think. - Listen empathetically. - Prepare them for changes as soon as possible. - Show how specific points tie into the big picture.	- Be prepared. - Be specific. - Go into considerable detail. - Provide accurate, factual evidence. - Give them space. - Give them time to make choices. - Get ready to listen to more information than you really wanted to know. - Follow up in writing.
DON'T	- Ramble. - Lose things. - Chit chat. - Make decisions for them. - Get off track.	- Be impersonal. - Be too businesslike. - Talk down to them.	- Answer questions for them. - Be abrupt and fast. - Threaten or demand. - Question their loyalty. - Expect them to cope well with hostility or disapproval.	- Be disorganized. - Force decisions. - Get emotional. - Be vague.
PACE	Fast/Decisive	Fast/Spontaneous	Slow/Easy	Slow/Systematic
STRESS REACTION	Dictate/Assert	Attack/Be Sarcastic	Submit/Acquiesce	Withdraw/Avoid

	LIONS	**PEACOCKS**	**DOVES**	**TURTLES**
SELLING AN IDEA	Focus on how your way of doing things will help them have better control.	Focus on how your way of doing things will help them influence others.	Focus on how your way of doing things will help them keep their environment stable.	Focus on your track record. Prepare statistics and backup materials.
RECRUITING ONTO A TEAM AND COACHING	Wants to earn according to individual effort, work quickly and independently, wants challenges, financial incentives, and specific milestones at which to aim.	Likes stories about how others have succeeded, opportunities for special recognition, flexible schedules, and occasions to be the center of attention.	Likes a warm, friendly, team-building organization, does well in face to face contact, needs one-on-one supervision and access to supervisor for discussions.	Wants stable, goal-oriented organization, loves to be trained, needs evidence that the organization and plan have a proven formula for success.
DESCRIBING BENEFITS	ACTION and SPEED Efficiency Savings Profit Bottom Line Results	FUN and EXCITEMENT Focus on how they will be perceived for making the decision for going with your idea, product, or service.	FAMILY ATMOSPHERE Predictable Reliable Steady	STRUCTURE Accurate Logic Quality Precise
NEEDS	High goals, recognition with financial rewards, fast results.	Popularity, team enthusiasm, appreciation, and to be creative.	May neglect goals for sake of good relationships, will enjoy telling personal stories and anecdotes.	To him/her strength is logical, problem-solving ability, everything should be in its place, perfectionist.
WANTS TO BE...	In Charge	Admired	Liked	Correct
IRRITATED BY...	Inefficiency Indecision	Boredom Routine	Insensitivity Impatience	Surprises Unpredictability

IF WHAT YOU HAVE TRIED DOES NOT WORK. DON'T GIVE UP!

TRY SOMETHING ELSE.

Technical Information

The Communication Jungle Has an Appropriate Database

The Communication Jungle assessment has proven itself to be a valuable tool again and again. It has been successfully used with thousands of people of diverse ages and backgrounds since 2003. It has been used to improve workplace interactions in a multitude of industries and has been used effectively in jobs ranging from individual contributors to high level executives.

The current analysis of *The Communication Jungle* database was performed in August 2009.

The Communication Jungle is Reliable

Reliability refers to how replicable the results of the assessment are likely to be. Cronbach's Alpha coefficient was calculated for this analysis. An Alpha reliability coefficient of 1.00 represents perfect internal consistency, while an alpha of 0.00 represents a total lack of consistency. According to the American Psychological Association, reliabilities above .70 are acceptable, while values above .80 are considered very good. The reliabilities for *The Communication Jungle* dimensions range from .80 to .87, which are all very good.

The Communication Jungle is Valid

Validity refers to the degree to which *The Communication Jungle* assessment measures what it is intended to measure. There are several types of validity that are particularly relevant to *The Communication Jungle*.

Content validity refers to the degree to which the items are consistent with peoples' beliefs about the characteristics reflected by the items. Hundreds of participants have indicated their agreement that the items reflect the styles that are measured on the assessment and that those styles accurately portray their modes of interacting with others. Information from a variety of sources including assessment participants, subject matter experts on communication and the interpersonal interaction literature was synthesized into *The Communication Jungle* assessment model. Thus a number of different sources were used to establish the content validity of the assessment.

Construct validity refers to the degree to which the assessment measures unitary and meaningful concepts. Construct validity can be demonstrated by:

- Factor analysis
- Internal consistency analysis
- Correlations among styles

The results of the factor analysis demonstrated that *The Communication Jungle* items grouped together in the anticipated manner. Based on a two-factor solution, the great majority of the items in the assessment strongly loaded with the hypothesized dimension. These results support the structure of *The Communication Jungle* model and indicate the items on the assessment are suitable for measuring the model.

The internal consistency analysis is reflected by the Cronbach's Alpha results reported earlier. All of the coefficients are above .70. Those results also provide strong support that the items for the individual dimensions are treated as homogeneous constructs by the respondents and therefore adequately describe the concepts being measured.

Furthermore, *The Communication Jungle* Assessment model postulates that styles which are opposites such as Lion and Dove or Peacock and Turtle will have strong negative correlations. On the other hand dimensions which are hypothesized to be parallel will have weak to moderate correlations. This was supported. In other words, strong negative correlations are observed between Lion and Dove (-.787), and between Peacock and Turtle (-.813). On the other hand, relatively weak correlations are observed between parallel pairs of dimensions such as Lion and Peacock (-.017), as well as Dove and Turtle (.293).

Order Additional Copies

Additional guides may be purchased at Amazon.com. For wholesale orders, contact us at info@fullcourtpresspublishing.com.

Take the Instrument Online

The Communication Jungle is available online at www.communicationjungle.com.

Take the Multi-Rater Instrument Online

To take *The Communication Jungle* as a multi-rater instrument where others can share their perception of your behavior, visit www.communicationjungle.com.

The multi-rater tool is only available online.

Made in the USA
Charleston, SC
11 August 2015